NEW
KITCHEN
IDEA BOOK

JOANNE KELLAR BOUKNIGHT

The Taunton Press

To Neilie and Sebastian

The Taunton Press
Inspiration for hands-on living®

The Taunton Press, Inc., 63 South Main Street, PO Box 5506, Newtown, CT 06470-5506
e-mail: tp@taunton.com

New Kitchen Idea Book was originally published in hardcover
in 2004 by The Taunton Press, Inc.

EDITOR: Stefanie Ramp
JACKET DESIGN: Jeannet Leendertse
INTERIOR DESIGN: Lori Wendin
LAYOUT: Cathy Cassidy
ILLUSTRATOR: Christine Erikson
COVER PHOTOGRAPHERS: Front cover, top row (left to right): © Jason McConathy; © 2004 carolynbates.com;
© carolynbates.com; Charles Miller © The Taunton Press, Inc.; second row: © 2004 carolynbates.com;
Amy Albert © The Taunton Press, Inc.; © 2004 carolynbates.com; Amy Albert © The Taunton Press, Inc.;
third row: Amy Albert © The Taunton Press, Inc.; Photo courtesy Kennebec Company, photo by Steve Fazio;
© Jason McConathy; © Jason McConathy; Back cover, top: © Jason McConathy; bottom row (left to right):
© Randy O'Rourke; © 2004 carolynbates.com; © Alise O'Brien photography

Taunton Home® is a trademark of the Taunton Press, Inc.,
registered in the U.S. Patent and Trademark Office.

Library of Congress Cataloging-in-Publication Data

Bouknight, Joanne Kellar.
  New kitchen idea book / Joanne Bouknight.
      p. cm.
  ISBN-13: 978-1-56158-642-4I hardcover
  ISBN-10: 1-56158-642-0 hardcover
  ISBN-13: 978-1-56158-693-6 paperback
  ISBN-10: 1-56158-693-5 paperback
  1. Kitchens--Design and construction. I. Title.
TX653.B69 2004
643'.3--dc22
                          2003020534

Printed in the United States of America
10 9 8

The following manufacturers/names appearing in the New Kitchen Idea Book are trademarks: Medex™

Acknowledgments

The number of people who had a hand in this book would take up much more space than allowed, so I'll have to amend my long list. My thanks again to Taunton Press, which continues to combine art and function in all its publications. When writing this book turned out to be a pain in the neck (thanks to a pinched nerve), Carolyn Mandarano, Maria Taylor, and Stefanie Ramp were especially generous with time and editorial direction, and Robyn Aitken was gracious when time ran short. Thanks to the *Fine Homebuilding* editor/photographer/fine-house zealots who each took time out to answer questions. Thanks, too, to Amy Albert at *Fine Cooking* for access to her great kitchen photos. Many designers, builders, craftspeople, and homeowners are responsible for these kitchens (and I'm happy to say these are all *real* kitchens). My great thanks to all of you.

For advice, insight, and details, special thanks to Diane Morgan, Flo Braker, Anne Otterson, Alan Bouknight of Azzarone Contracting Corp., Laura Kaehler and Joeb Moore of Kaehler Moore Architects, David Lyon of Cooleen Horner Kitchens Bath Tile Stone, and Cynthia Canaday, Peter Bentel, Paul Bentel, and Carol Bentel of Bentel + Bentel Architects. Many thanks to photographers Carolyn Bates, Jason McConathy, Brian Vanden Brink, and Durston Saylor.

Once again, my patient and accommodating friends and family tolerated my schedule for months. Again—and again—my husband Neil not only filled in for me in so many ways but was willing to discuss everything kitchen, from subfloors to Sub-Zeros. And finally, our sons Neilie and Sebastian have been remarkably understanding and good-humored. By necessity, they are learning to cook, starting with the basic food groups of quesadillas and brownies. Thanks, guys.

Contents

Introduction

When my mother-in-law, Doris Azzarrone, was a girl in Flushing, Queens, her father Louis built a house to her mother's specifications. Tess was adamant: Two kitchens were better than one. A formal kitchen was built on the main living level while a canning kitchen was built on the ground floor off the herb garden. This was the down-and-dirty kitchen, with a big range, a refrigerator, tile countertops and backsplashes, and a white-painted concrete floor with a drain in the middle.

Tess also used the downstairs kitchen for messy foods such as roasts, fish, and long-cooking sauces. On Sunday afternoons the clinking of pot lids from downstairs would indicate the arrival of future son-in-law O'Neil Bouknight, taking a peek at dinner. Tess approved of Neil because he, too, came from the countryside (she from Campagna, Italy, and he from South Carolina) and because he loved home cooking, unlike her four city-born daughters (Doris included), who turned up their noses at their mother's delicious home-spun cooking, now venerated as *cucina rustica*. "*You* don't know what's good," Tess would say.

How wonderful it would be to have a waterproof, stainproof space like that canning kitchen—one that you could just hose down after cooking. But many of us don't work at home the way Tess did, sewing, keeping house, and cooking.

When we do make meals, we want to be surrounded by family or friends. And we multitask—work on the computer, do bills, grade papers, monitor homework. Our ideal kitchen must be not only functional like that canning kitchen, but beautiful as well, like the upstairs kitchen. It *is* possible to achieve that blend of beauty and utility, as you'll see the kitchens in this book. Design basics kick off the book, with subsequent chapters moving through each of the major elements of kitchens: cabinets, shelves and pantries, countertops and sinks, cooking and cooling appliances, and lighting.

It's easy to spend days, weeks, or months, choosing surfaces—your kitchen's fashionable side—but also spend time choosing the things that will make your kitchen work. You love that slender gooseneck faucet, but are you willing to have another hole cut in the countertop (and more to clean around) for a separate sprayer? And what about hyperpractical issues, such as switchplates? If fixture types are switched separately, for instance—advisable for flexible lighting—you may end up with a formidable row of switches. This book will help you navigate the proper balance of form and function with its hundreds of photos supplemented by nitty-gritty information collected in drawings and sidebars.

Another word of advice: Be watchful of the latest thing. Any new, hot material will have new, not-so-hot providers and installers. Do research, follow up recommendations, and don't be swayed only by the bottom line. Take fashion for what it is—fleeting. Choose what works for you, whether it's an appliance or a finish. Your choice of an uncommon countertop material may turn up in next year's "hot new trends" kitchen magazine. Durability is important, but you can replace a less-durable countertop three times over for the price of a countertop that's as tough as nails. Keep in mind that most home lenders suggest limiting a kitchen renovation to 15 percent of the home's value. On the other hand, it's *your* kitchen, and you may be working in it for a lifetime. Ideally, you've hired a contractor you trust. If so, hover lightly. Many contractors would love their clients to travel to Antarctica during construction. Make sure that you and your contractor agree about who is responsible for what. Understand that undergoing a kitchen renovation can be an emotional roller coaster, when every choice is fraught with what-ifs, every hitch seems like a calamity, and every meal is fast food. But your kitchen *will* be finished. When it's finished, stop second-guessing your decisions. Live with your new kitchen before declaring that the color of your granite countertops is an utter disaster. In a week or two, chances are you'll love it.

Kitchen Design: From Looks to Layout

Considering how much time is spent in the kitchen, shouldn't it be the most gorgeous room in the house, with the most sumptuous materials, finishes, and fixtures? Well, that's becoming the case with modern kitchens. Many of today's showcase kitchens boast fine cabinetry that rivals the furniture in an English castle and flooring as intricate and durable as that in an Italian church. Even the everyday kitchen is evolving into a high-tech and highly aesthetic space.

We want our kitchens to work well and we also want them to look good, but the beauty of a kitchen depends on more than just the finishing touches. Consider the bare bones of the kitchen, and make a space that's bright, well proportioned, and, above all, comfortable and easy to use.

If you are remodeling, the most bang for your buck will come from connecting the kitchen to the rest of the house, which better suits the modern lifestyle. This, along with configuring the kitchen to maximize efficiency, will ensure a space that provides both pleasure and convenience.

◄ A KITCHEN WITH SERIOUS APPLIANCES CAN BE EQUALLY as whimsical with a mix of beautifully designed materials. This kitchen was loosely based on a circus theme, with harlequin tiles, charmed-snake pulls, and multiple colors. It's a refined circus, with muted colors of similar value, and stainless steel is the metal finish of choice throughout. Cabinets are stained or natural maple, cherry, beech, and English sycamore.

▶ THIS CEDAR-LOG HOUSE ON THE OREGON COAST is fitted with a small, modern kitchen. The kitchen and built-ins are streamlined, with flush overlay cabinet doors, recessed shelving, and the refrigerator faced with the paneling.

▼ HERE'S A KITCHEN WITH TRADITIONAL DETAILS and a few unusual twists on convention. Doors and drawers are inset and paneled and fitted with traditional butt hinges, which require more precision to install than adjustable hinges.

SET THE STYLE

All the parts of a kitchen work together to create a look, so you will want to consider carefully the design of cabinetry and hardware, flooring, wall and ceiling surfaces, appliances, countertops, and lighting.

The kitchens you'll see here run the style gamut, from sedate to hyper, colonial to contemporary. Kitchens classified as traditional include country style, rustic style, Craftsman style—any style that reflects the past or our nostalgic view of the past. Moldings, hardware, and light fixtures tend to be detailed or even ornate. Contemporary kitchens tend toward more streamlined surfaces and hardware and flush joinery, and are often glossier than traditional-style kitchens, though that's not a rule.

◄ A KITCHEN DESIGNED FOR MAJOR MEAL MAKING can be pretty, too. The matching freezer and refrigerator mean business, and a warming oven anchors the big island. Two sinks make it easy for two to work. The window behind the sink is set back, allowing space for a mini greenhouse on the sill.

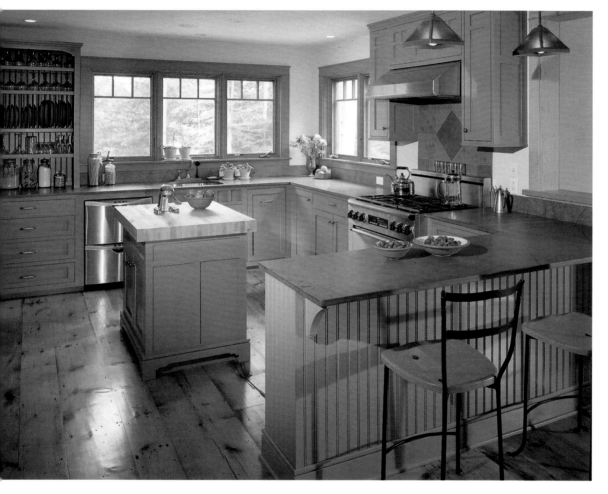

◄ CABINETS LOOK TRADITIONAL WITH THEIR MUTED BLUE-GREEN COLOR, inset paneled doors and drawers, and bases articulated to look like furniture with legs. The peninsula is paneled with traditional beadboard and the countertops are slate. But stainless-steel appliances—dishwasher drawers, professional-style range, and built-in refrigerator—keep up to date, along with brushed-silver pulls.

Of course, take a close look at most kitchens and you'll see that they are actually eclectic, with a mix of traditional detailing and contemporary layouts, lighting, or finishes. Like clothing styles, the latest kitchen styles are generated by designers and manufacturers who'd like you to think that your kitchen is hopelessly out of date. The drawback of leaning heavily on the latest fashions is that a kitchen can look outdated in 10 years—or less. The upside is that it's often easy to make a dramatic transformation: Just changing hardware, paint colors, and accessories can add plenty of style to a tired kitchen.

▲ A KITCHEN IN THE VEIN OF THE EUROPEAN FARMHOUSE KITCHEN has rich, rustic finishes. Tile floors, stone walls, and a massive kitchen table are paired with a massive French range and ceiling-mounted pendants.

Traditional Kitchens

Traditional kitchens have in common a prevalence of natural materials and articulated details, as opposed to the high-tech materials and sleek detailing commonly found in modern-style kitchens. A generic traditional kitchen will have wood or stone floors, natural or painted wood cabinets, and stone, tile, or wood countertops—or a synthetic countertop material that looks like stone. Hinges may be exposed and moldings may be elaborate.

If your heart is set on a particular historic style, study the details and colors found in

houses from that day. If you are leaning toward a Craftsman-style kitchen, for example, you may want to go for exposed wood beams, oak cabinets, and moss-green tiles. Take it a step further and make those oak cabinets quartersawn with flat-panel doors. Pendant Craftsman-style light fixtures, oak flooring, built-ins, and burnished brass hardware in the appropriate style will complete the look of a Craftsman-period kitchen. Read up on historical styles to find ideas for details, colors, finishes, and sources for refurbished or reproduction fittings, appliances, and cabinetry. A good

▲ THIS SUNNY, COUNTRY-STYLE KITCHEN IS THE ESSENCE of leisurely life, with gathered curtains and cabinet panels, scalloped wall-cabinet rail, and built-in china cabinet. Beadboard in panels, on walls, and on the ceiling are clues that this house is in the country— beachside, in this case.

◄ THIS ISN'T A TRADITIONAL KITCHEN IN TERMS OF LAYOUT or placement in a space, but the cabinets are traditional, with inset paneled doors, and the beadboard is a time-honored wall surface in century-old beach houses. Bead-board was used as a wall finish in unheated houses in lieu of plaster.

basic guide to kitchen and house styles is included on the Kitchen.com Web site, the Internet company of the kitchen and bath industry (also see the Sources section on p. 186).

Of course, it is possible to mix modern elements with traditional details. In fact, today's traditional-style kitchen rarely forgoes space-age appliances and accessories for stylistic purity. The trick is to recreate the atmosphere of your favorite style—cozy and filled with home-baked pies, for instance— without giving up on conveniences like single-lever faucets and convection ovens.

▶ IN THIS MODERN HOUSE IN VENICE, CALIFORNIA, space flows keeping the kitchen and dining space open to light and air from a huge operable skylight above. Joints between materials are flush, the structure is often exposed, and geometric shapes are assembled asymmetrically, all hallmarks of modern design.

▼ THIS CONTEMPORARY KITCHEN FITS NEATLY INTO THE CORNER of a white great room, designated by an island that's painted gray. Corner cabinets are simply detailed with flush-overlay frosted-glass panels. A custom-made, white-paneled steel plate is hung from the ceiling to call out the edge of the kitchen and to provide task and ambient lighting.

Modern-style Kitchens

The hallmark of a modern-style kitchen—you can also call it a contemporary kitchen—is sleek detailing, and it's back in fashion again. It doesn't matter if materials are wood, stone, tile, or the latest high-tech, factory-made synthetic. What matters is how the materials are finished and how they are joined. Rather than using moldings to cover joints, joints are left visible, often with a reveal (a narrow slot) between materials. Modern style can require more meticulous craftsmanship, as it's harder to make two materials flush than to cover their edges with a molding.

Eclectic Kitchens

If you want to get technical about it, most of us have eclectic kitchens: We mix styles without being bothered by convention. Your kitchen may incorporate both wood countertops and stainless-steel backsplashes, but you consider your kitchen traditional. Or you don't think twice about using recessed downlights in a Craftsman-style bungalow kitchen. Strictly speaking, we use the term "eclectic" to describe those kitchens that employ purposeful juxtapositions of modern and traditional styles, or to describe kitchens that are simply whimsical. An artfully eclectic kitchen may take many months—or years—to attain just the right look.

▲ THIS CHEERFUL FAMILY KITCHEN IS A LIVELY PLACE, with red chairs and red backsplash tile, a cluster of colored pans and pots hanging near the range, and bright white cabinets. These basic overlay cabinets are topped with small cabinets reserved for seasonal and lesser-used gear.

◀ THESE BLUE-PAINTED CABINETS ARE TRADITIONALLY STYLED with elaborate paneled doors, but the cabinets are flush overlay rather than inset. The heavy wood Dutch door and the stone tile floor recall old European kitchens, but the smoothtop cooktop and inset sinks add a contemporary look.

▲ THIS IS AN INSPIRED WAY TO FINISH
off the edge of a handsome
kitchen. The cabinetry turns the
corner at the right, and that's
where special dishware is stored.
The countertop is raised, perfect
for a buffet layout yet high
enough to hide kitchen debris.

▶ THIS KITCHEN OPENS TO THE
SECOND FLOOR and is highlighted
by skylights shining over a grid of
beams. The beams not only frame
the kitchen space but carry the
pendant lights over the island.
The kitchen steps down to a cozy
family room with a fireplace and a
lowered ceiling.

FITTING THE KITCHEN INTO THE HOUSE

A kitchen sees the most action of any room in the house, so there's no question that it requires a close connection with living spaces. How the kitchen meets the rest of the house is your choice, from a framed opening with a door to no separation at all. For a step beyond the basic door, the tried-and-true passthrough allows food, if not people, to move from kitchen to dining room. Or use base and wall cabinets—opaque or transparent—to buffer the kitchen from living or dining spaces. This provides convenient storage for dishes, especially if doors open from both sides. Connect the kitchen with the rest of the house by making space for activities that have nothing to do with cooking, such as working at a computer or doing arts and crafts.

▲ A KITCHEN DOESN'T HAVE TO DRESS IN THE LATEST STYLE to be well designed. This is a delightful way to set off a kitchen in a small house or apartment—as a pavilion with columns and an entablature. The plastic-laminate-capped walls are the ideal height for hungry onlookers to lean on.

◄ THIS KITCHEN HAS TWO PARTS: THE SERIOUS workspace in the background and the serving area with eating space in the foreground. This bar also serves as the mail-sorting center, with cubbies built into the adjacent cabinet.

▲ THE STAIR PULLS THE KITCHEN AND DINING SPACE TOGETHER and makes them the center of attention. There are certainly plenty of places to sit, from the table to the island countertop to a built-in bench to the side.

▶ THIS KITCHEN FITS INTO HALF OF A BIG ROOM SEAMLESSLY, in part because it takes on the detailing of the stair, which is a major element in the space. Cabinetry and stair are paneled to match.

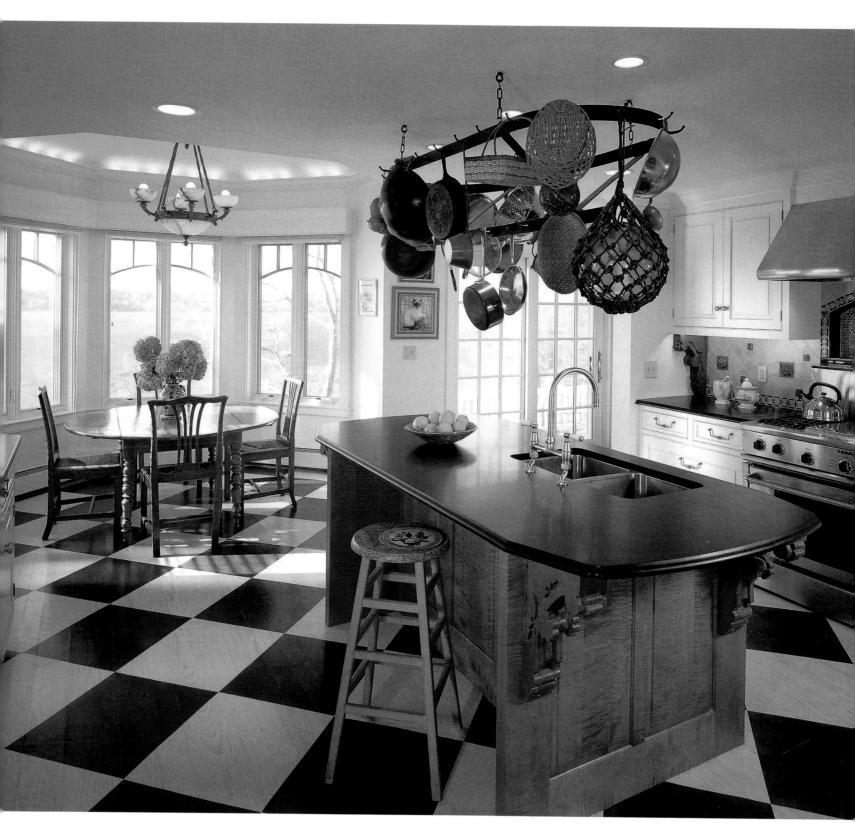

▲ THIS DINING AREA IS CALLED OUT BY AN OCTAGONAL coved ceiling with perimeter lighting, a handsome pendant light fixture, and windows on four sides. It would be hard to find a view to match this one. Multilight sliding doors allow for quick access to the great outdoors. The wood floor is painted with a diamond pattern that enlarges and enlivens the space.

▲ THIS KITCHEN IS LAID OUT TO SUIT A PROFESSIONAL BAKER. The rolling cart is topped with a butcher-block work surface and provides storage and cooling space. Multiple cooking sources are clustered at one end, joined by a professional-grade refrigerator.

▶ THERE'S A MAIN CIRCULATION ROUTE RIGHT THROUGH THIS KITCHEN, from the breakfast nook (where the photo was taken) to the dining room. The food preparation and cooking workspace is all on the left so noncooks can steer clear. The refrigerator is at the edge of the workspace for easy access.

CONFIGURING THE KITCHEN

One person's perfect kitchen workspace may be another person's kitchen nightmare. A crackerjack cook may fume when family members trespass, or may be happier with a sous-chef or two. A so-so cook may welcome helping hands in the workspace or may shoo onlookers away to work in peace. Two cooks in the kitchen will demand two substantial workspaces, ideally with two sinks, not necessarily of the same size or purpose.

Consider how food is cooked in your kitchen. The cook's paths among the important nodes should not be so long that cooking, serving, and cleaning up are chores. If cooktop pyrotechnics is your sport, make the cooktop easy to work around by providing

Universal Design Is for Everyone

HERE'S A TWIST ON THE USUAL COUNTERTOP DINING: The eating surface is at regular table height—about 30 in.—which allows for both standard chairs and wheelchair use. Aisles and doorways are wide and the dining space is at the same level as the terrace, making circulation easy for everyone.

UNIVERSAL DESIGN is a term coined to cover all kinds of design, from tools to airports, but it is especially appropriate to our kitchens, where easy access is always appreciated. The goal is to create tools and spaces that are flexible, easy to use, relatively goof-proof, and easy to maneuver in by everyone, not just the able-bodied. Most features of universal design are pure common sense. Keep pantry and refrigerator near where groceries are unloaded, and make the path taken by food items short and direct. Make aisles wide enough for comfort, but not too wide for efficiency—42 in. to 48 in.

Provide a variety of countertop heights for sitting or standing. Anyone with back problems should consider making counters higher than the standard 36 in., which allows for less bending, particularly at the sink. Locate most kitchen storage between 20 in. and 44 in. above the floor, and fit your kitchen with a sturdy stepstool for accessing the higher, seasonal stuff. Shallow shelves are easier to access than deep cabinets, or provide full-extension drawers or pull-out shelves. Bypass those teeny-weeny button pulls in favor of levers or wire pulls, which are much easier to handle. A side-by-side refrigerator is easier to access overall, or go for refrigerator and freezer drawers. Likewise, a drawer-style dishwasher is easy on the back. Single-lever faucets are much easier to operate than two-handled versions, and a pull-out hose is ideal for everyone.

And don't forget lighting, regardless of whether you have eagle eyes or limited vision. A dim kitchen is not only depressing but dangerous, so install abundant under-cabinet lighting as well as overall lighting to make cooking a delight rather than a chore.

ample counterspace on each side and across the aisle for food preparation and serving. A sink should be reasonably close to make it easy to drain pasta or transfer a colander of green beans to a pot. While it's essential, the hulking refrigerator doesn't have to be in the center of the workspace. Positioning the fridge at the outskirt of the workspace—near dining, preferably—will keep thirsty onlookers from interfering with cooks.

The Kitchen Island

It's hard to find a new kitchen today that doesn't have an island, descendant of the big farm worktable. Today's island is often more than a table: It's a minikitchen in itself, with cabinets below and a pot rack above, a seating area at one end and a cooktop or sink at another end.

An island can be free-floating, such as a butcher-block cart, in which case there's no concern for electrical or gas connections. If an island is fixed in place, chances are it will require electrical outlets.

▲ THIS CURVED ISLAND—the granite countertop is a long oval and the oiled teak countertop is biscotti-shaped—defines the border between the linear kitchen and the dining area, which itself faces a salt marsh. Its front is faced with cherry beadboard. The three pendant lights and their curved support reinforce the shape of the island.

▶ THIS BEEFY ISLAND IS AN AMALGAM OF A WOOD Lutyens-style kitchen table and white-painted English cabinetry, with a substantial plinth in place of a kickspace. The straight end of the island is used for seating, while cabinets below provide storage for cookware and serving pieces.

◄ RATHER THAN CANTILEVER THE COUNTERTOP to make an unencumbered stretch of eating space, the designer supported the countertop on two tall cabinets that act like beefy legs. These cabinets also provide extra storage space for dishes.

▼ THERE'S A CHOICE OF SEATING IN THIS COMFORTABLE KITCHEN, from the built-in bench to the small breakfast table with green chairs. A lowered ceiling soffit provides a sense of shelter, as well as space for ductwork.

A Place to Eat

It's a rare kitchen that doesn't have at least one seat for informal dining. Many of us eat breakfast, lunch, and everyday dinners in the kitchen, and may even prefer a single dining space for all meals in or next to the kitchen. Keys to an enjoyable eating place are close proximity to cooking and serving, an agreeable view, the right lighting, and comfortable seating—whether freestanding or built-in.

Take Measure: Laying Out a Kitchen

THESE DAYS THE CLASSIC KITCHEN TRIANGLE—forged between range, sink, and refrigerator—has exploded into a more complex geometry. The modern kitchen often boasts a second cook, the range may be bifurcated into wall ovens and a cooktop, and two sinks have become the rule. That's not counting the microwave, separate refrigerator and freezer units, or even multiple refrigerator drawers dispersed to different parts of the kitchen. Finally, the ubiquitous island has made the triangle a little more complicated to lay out, but it has made it easier to provide space for extra appliances, such as second sinks and a refrigerator drawer for drinks.

But no matter: While the classic kitchen triangle is suggested to be between 12 ft. and 26 ft. overall, the goal is to keep the tasks of food preparation, serving, and cleanup efficient and easy. Even if you've got a kitchen the size of a

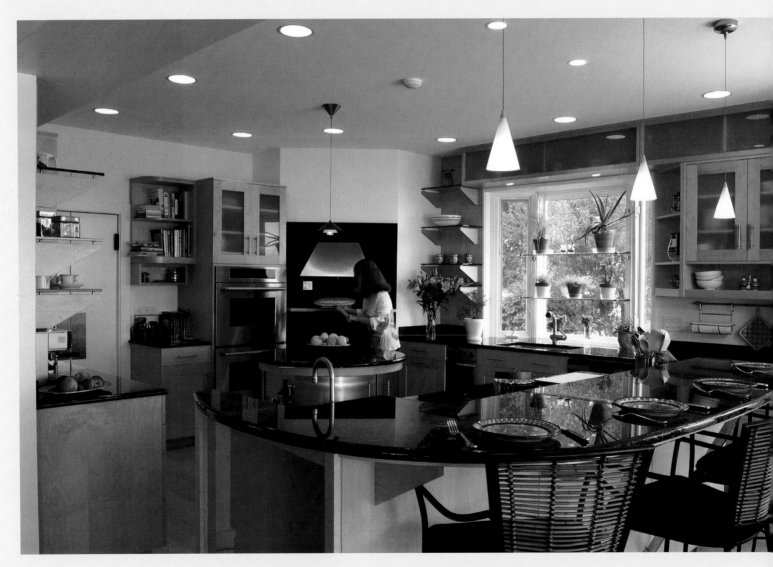

▲ THIS KITCHEN KEEPS TWO COOKS AND SEVERAL ONLOOKERS happy by the intelligent use of countertop space. The cooktop has two landing spaces as well as a serving countertop to its right, while the baker uses the small round island for food prep and for setting hot pans from wall ovens and the much-used wood-fired brick oven.

football field, cluster your major appliances so that you don't wear yourself out making a meal.

An always solo cook in a galley kitchen will love a 38-in.-wide aisle, but in any kitchen with multiple inhabitants—cooks or not—the aisle should be at least 42 in. and up to 48 in. for two cooks. This allows drawers, dishwasher, and refrigerator to be opened with ease, and allows two busy people to pass each other. Add more room if the aisle backs up on a seating area.

A caveat for a two-person kitchen: Don't locate the main garbage pail under the sink, as the sink is almost always in use. Put a garbage or compost container where you prepare food for cooking so that you don't have to scoop handfuls of peels and trimmings across the kitchen. Above all, try to steer noncooking traffic around—not through—the workspace.

Compactor

0 1 2 4 ft.

DW

Wood-burning stove

Wall ovens

Small island

Large island

Drawers below

Dining room

Laundry/pantry

▲ THIS ONE-SIDED BANQUETTE WITH MOVEABLE SEATING provides dining space in a small getaway house. The tabletop—supported by two pedestals and a plate of sheet steel—is rigged to slide away from the banquette to make it easy for anyone to get in and out. The bench provides a storage drawer on one end.

2

Cabinetry: The Kitchen Workhorse

Cabinetry rules the kitchen roost. Cabinet style sets the tone for how a kitchen looks and cabinet layout makes all the difference in how a kitchen functions. And how much cabinets cost establishes your kitchen budget—up to 70 percent in remodels. Whether remodeling or starting from scratch, choose cabinets early on, as that decision affects how long the job takes and sets the stage for choosing flooring, countertops, appliances, and a score of other elements.

Take advantage of the countless cabinet configurations available, mixing and matching types and styles if you wish. Arm yourself with a basic knowledge of the interrelated parts that make up cabinets, including cases, doors, drawers, and hardware. Then dive into the array of options for door and drawer styles, materials, and colors. Browse home-design magazines and the Internet as a start, then visit local kitchen-design shops and home centers, and take kitchen tours. After pinning down style choices, look inside cabinets—online, on paper, or in a shop—to discover the amazing array of accessories that can make your final choice of cabinets work most efficiently.

◄ THESE ELEGANT, CREAMY-WHITE PAINTED CABINETS were custom built to fit this tall room, reaching from floor to ceiling. Multipiece cornice molding makes a smooth transition between cabinet tops and ceiling, while a bull-nose trim and a valence conceals light fixtures. Base cabinets were given false legs to look like unfitted cabinets.

Cabinet Anatomy

ACH PART OF A CABINET CONTRIBUTES to its overall style and function. First, there's the basic box, called the case. Cases are built either as face-frame cabinets or frameless cabinets. Face-frame cabinets are traditionally American and are still the most popular style manufactured. A frame of horizontal rails and vertical stiles covers the exposed edge of the case and contributes significantly to its strength. Doors can either be set into the frame or overlay it.

A frameless cabinet—born in Europe in the 1950s to speed production and conserve wood—acquires strength from a thicker case and hence requires no stiffening face frame. A frameless cabinet is a simple box, and its doors and drawers nearly cover the case completely. Frameless cabinets have long been associated with modern styles, but today's frameless cabinets can easily be made to look traditional with panels and molding.

▼ CABINETS PLAY A MAJOR ROLE IN THIS KITCHEN, from the two-story wall cabinets and stacked-drawer base cabinets to the phalanx of ceiling-hung cabinets over the island. These are smartly backed with translucent panels to allow light to shine into the kitchen workspace. A continuous shelf under the eating counter is a handy addition that allows easy access to cookbooks, linens, or even homework.

THESE FRAMELESS CABINETS HAVE FLAT-SLAB DOORS and drawers, each with veneer carefully positioned to show off the figure of the wood.

THIS WALL CABINET IN A FARM-HOUSE KITCHEN is a truly traditional face-frame case, which doesn't need a back for strength.

FRAMELESS EURO-STYLE CABINETS LIKE THESE FREQUENTLY have a tall toespace. The flush overlay doors and drawers feature a shallow frame-and-panel design for subtle contrast. Cabinets stop short of the ceiling to leave a reveal.

Cabinet Sources

▲ ELABORATE CABINET MOLDINGS embellish tops and edges of these semi-custom cabinets.

◀ THE INSET DRAWERS IN THIS ISLAND face away from the busy workspace, making it easier for the designated table setter to access cutlery and linens. The cherry cabinetry is hand rubbed for a traditional look.

KITCHEN CABINETS CAN COME FROM MANY SOURCES, from a one-person shop to a multiacre factory. They vary greatly in price, depending on whether they're custom, stock, or something in between, but there's a wide range of options now available for every budget.

Stock cabinets are the most basic cabinet choice, and they are available off the shelf or within a few weeks from home centers and lumberyards or through a kitchen-products dealer or contractor. The cabinets can be installed by the dealer, a contractor, or you. Stock cabinets are built as individual components in standard sizes and increments, so filler pieces may be required to cover gaps between cabinet cases. Styles, finishes, hardware, and accessories vary widely, but can't be customized. Understandably, stock cabinets are about half the cost of many custom-manufactured cabinets.

Semicustom and custom cabinet manufacturers also offer a fixed but wide range of styles, finishes, hardware, accessories, sizes, and configurations, but the range of choices is much broader and there's wiggle room for custom-made pieces. Quality is generally very good to premium; delivery takes two to twelve weeks. Semicustom cabinets have fewer available options and cost about 25-percent less than cabinets from custom manufacturers.

Of course, you can hire a cabinetmaker to build custom cabinets, with or without the help of an architect or kitchen designer. Shop-built cabinets can be built in larger sections to fit specific site-measured situations. Shop-built cabinets generally take longer than manufactured cabinets—from six to twenty weeks—but not always. The shop will install the cabinets. Don't be shy about obtaining and querying the references that a potential cabinetmaker gives you. When ordering cabinets, ask for plans and elevations of the specific cabinetry, and request—or prepare for yourself—a list that calls out each cabinet, its accessories, and its hardware.

▲ THIS COLONIAL-STYLE HUTCH IS BUILT FROM HAND-PLANED PINE that's stained a walnut color. The cabinet case is face-frame, and each drawer is inset into the face frame. The outside edge of the cabinet is beaded, and shelves have multiple beads for a subtle contrast.

▲ IT TOOK CLEVER DESIGN WORK TO FIT THE CABINETS IN THIS CORNER, with typical wall-hung cabinets at right butting into a china-cabinet-style wall cabinet at left. Doors and drawers are inset into beaded face frames, and cabinet hardware is nickel plated, from door knobs to bin pulls to butt hinges.

▶ A MIX OF THE TRADITIONAL AND THE CONTEMPORARY, these cabinets have inset frame-and-panel doors without a center post and a beadboard backsplash. The wall of built-in cabinetry acts as pantry storage.

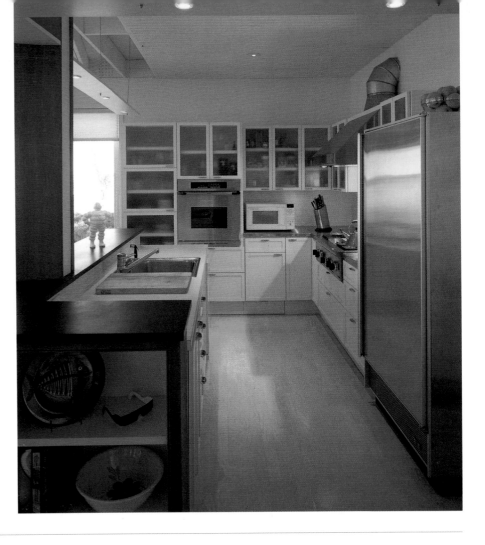

▶ THESE MODULAR FRAMELESS CABINETS COMBINE FRAME-AND-FLAT-PANEL doors and drawers in base cabinets with translucent-glass doors on wall cabinets. The European-height toe kick is about 9 in. high. The unusual proportion of the wide doors on the cabinets to the left of the wall oven provide visual interest to the bank of cabinetry.

BASIC CABINET TYPES

FRAMELESS CABINETS

Doors and drawers overlay the case completely (flush or full overlay).

Adjustable hinges are concealed when door is closed.

Frameless cabinet gets its strength from a stronger cabinet case.

Frameless cabinets usually have standard 4-in.-high toespaces; European-style frameless cabinets often have taller toespaces.

FACE-FRAME CABINET

A face frame slightly reduces size of opening, so drawers are smaller.

Traditional face-frame hinges are exposed and not adjustable, but concealed, adjustable hinges are available, too.

The face frame strengthens cabinet case.

Doors and drawers can be inset or overlay.

Sizing up Cabinets

MOST MANUFACTURED BASE CABINETS are just shy of 2 ft. deep and are 34½ in. high to receive a 1½ in. countertop; wall cabinets are 12 in. deep and 30 in. high. But that doesn't mean you can't customize your cabinets. Position them where they suit you best. For years the standard wall cabinet has been placed 16 in. to 18 in. above the countertop, but for a serious cook, or a tall one, this may not be high enough. More suitable may be a wall cabinet 24 in. above the countertop or even no wall cabinets at all, replaced instead by open shelves or a separate pantry, especially if the look is traditional. (Wall cabinets over sinks should be at least 30 in. above the countertop).

If you like deep countertops—say 30 in.—install standard 2-ft.-deep base cabinets 4 in. to 5 in. proud of the wall. The countertop will cover the gap in the back, but be sure to specify extradeep panels for any exposed cabinet sides so that there won't be a visible gap between cabinet and wall. Custom-built cabinets can certainly be specified at 30 in. deep, but deep cabinets are tougher to access, and 30-in. drawers require especially sturdy hardware and construction.

Custom-built wall cabinets can also be built taller to suit taller cooks or lower for bakers, who tend to prefer kneading and rolling out pastry with fully extended arms.

Another tack is to drop the wall cabinet all the way down to the countertop, creating a china-cabinet effect. Researchers say that the most useful storage space is between hip height and shoulder height, so a china cabinet dropped into the lineup of base cabinets may be more suitable than ordinary wall cabinets.

▲ KEEPING THE WALL CABINETS HIGH IN THIS KITCHEN makes it easier for a tall cook to use the sink. The frameless cabinets feature beadboard panels in flat frames. The big drawer under the wall oven handles pots.

▲ THESE FRAMELESS CABINET DOORS RUN STRAIGHT to the ceiling, with a slight reveal. The trim on the recessed ceiling light is as narrow as possible so that doors can swing freely.

Doors and Drawers

DOORS AND DRAWERS SET THE STYLE for a kitchen. Doors and drawers can be flat-slab (also called one-piece) or frame-and-panel; frames can be beaded, flat, or carved, and panels can be flat, beaded, raised, and more. In short, doors and drawers can take on any look you like.

Keep in mind that all doors and drawers on frameless cabinets must be full overlay (see drawing on p. 32) to cover the edge of the case. For face-frame cabinets, reveal overlay doors, which show part of the face frame, are the most common and least expensive style. Inset doors are more painstaking to make and hang than overlay doors, but are standard in historical styles.

As you choose drawer and door styles, consider hardware, too. Pulls, hinges, and drawer slides have a big impact on looks, cost, and durability. Some styles require a long lead time; order them in the early stages of design.

▲ IN THIS KITCHEN OF BLUE-STAINED CABINETRY, one face-frame case is fitted with wood runners and pull-out baskets for easy access to a few essentials.

◄ THESE UNIQUE CABINETS ARE A MIXTURE of opaque and transparent, allowing a limited view of the dining room through clear-glass upper cabinets and steel-mesh door panels on the backside that open into the dining room, allowing plates to go back and forth. This palette of bicolored framed doors and drawers makes cabinets that are both lively and tailored.

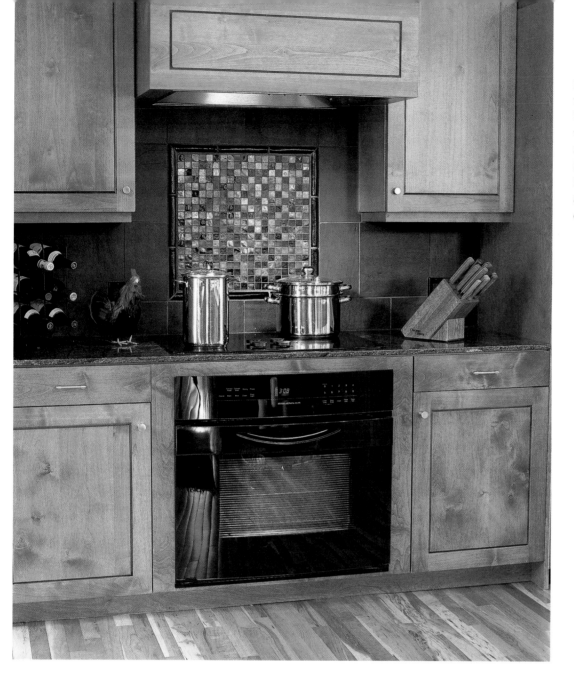

◀ THIS SYMMETRICAL COMPOSITION IS ANCHORED at each side by large, frame-and-flush-panel doors in both the wall and base cabinets, with the same panel design applied to the range hood. The homeowner liked the simpler look of doors, so pull-out shelves are used instead of stacks of drawers in the base cabinets.

▶ ROW UPON ROW OF APOTHECARY-STYLE DRAWERS are fitted with ring pulls for an unusual take on the basic base cabinet. The key here is to decide on a logical order for easy access, so you don't have to play a memory game with drawer contents.

A flat-slab or single-piece door is most often veneered.

V-groove boards with backing or edge-glued planks without frame

A flat-slab door with molding applied

Inset doors and drawers fit within the face frame.

Flat frame with recessed flat panel; often called Shaker or Colonial style

Extra wide flat frame with recessed panel

Beaded frame and panel; beading can be integral or applied and may be on the frame or panel.

Reveal overlay doors and drawers partially overlap the face frame.

Flat frame with beadboard; painted, stained, or natural

Frame with mitered corners and raised panel; frame and panel may be simple, as shown, or may be beaded, carved, or embellished in other ways.

Frame with glass panel; glass can be single- or multipaned, textured or clear.

Flush overlay doors and drawers cover a frameless cabinet case.

THIS WALL FULL OF FRAMELESS CABINETS with overlay doors makes a stunning counterpoint to the open shelves in the center. The wire pulls on the doors add an interesting rhythm to the wall. The stone tile floor matches the tone of the cabinets, giving the kitchen a serene ambience.

THIS WALL OF DISH CABINETRY IS BUILT with the traditional setup of solid cabinets at the base and glazed cabinets above. Drawers are overlay, while doors are inset with a frame-and-double-panel pattern that goes almost all the way to the floor. But the multipaned wall cabinets are the stars here, and beautifully proportioned.

▲ ▶ THESE HOMEOWNERS CAN HAVE THEIR BOOKS AND COOK, TOO. A
healthy collection of cookbooks is close at hand, yet there's still room
behind the piano-hinged swinging bookshelf for bulkier cooking tools
that aren't necessarily used every day.

THE SCULPTURAL HARDWARE ON THESE CABINETS has the presence of knobs but acts like pulls, as it takes a hooked finger to open doors and drawers. The reveals at the ceiling and toespace are black, visually connecting the cabinets, refrigerator, and countertop. The cabinets over the sink are recessed, making it more comfortable to use that workspace, while the textured-glass panels add sparkle to the colored glassware inside.

THESE FRAMELESS BEECH CABINETS ARE CAREFULLY COMPOSED and crafted to operate smoothly and look elegant. Edge pulls (seen on mirrored doors of built-in medicine cabinets) and cylinder pulls are stainless steel.

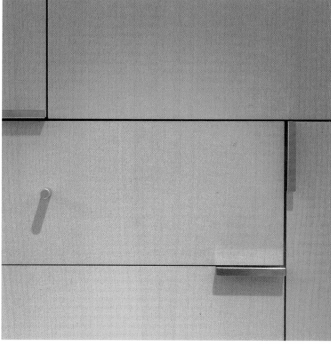

THIS KITCHEN CORNER IS COMPOSED to look good and take advantage of potentially lost space. Fixed dowels keep wine at hand in a narrow slot, while two doors—opening in opposite directions for different purposes—take the space next to the refrigerator.

▼ ▶ BECAUSE IT IS THE CENTERPIECE OF A BUSY KITCHEN, this island cabinet is round to smooth traffic flow. Curved stainless doors conceal goods on adjustable shelves, while the opposite side contains a drawer within a drawer. Curved doors, which are thin layers of poplar plywood clad with a stainless-steel skin, slide on custom-made track hardware. Interiors are veneered with maple.

A LOOK AT DRAWERS

A flat-slab drawer over a flat frame-and-panel door, inset in face-frame case

A drawer with beaded edge over a frame-and-raised-panel door, inset in face-frame case

A bank of same-size flat-slab drawers, overlaying a frame-less case

Graduated-size drawers with beaded edges, inset in face-frame case, with intermediate rails

Graduated-size drawers with beaded edges, inset in face-frame, but without intermediate rails

Drawer Slides

RAWERS ARE SUPPORTED BY, and glide on, slides (or glides). The industry standard for a good-quality drawer slide is a side-mounted, epoxy-coated (for reduced noise) steel slide with nylon rollers. Less-expensive slides are mounted at the lower edge of the drawer side, while heavy-duty slides fit on the side. Heavy-duty ball bearings last longer and are more stable than nylon rollers, but they also cost more.

Full-extension slides add to cost, but many designers automatically specify them because they expose the contents of the entire drawer to view when opened. They are essential for big pot and pan drawers. To save money, consider using full-extension slides on just the top drawers. Self-closing drawer slides allow the drawer to shut automatically when it is 3 in. or 4 in. from the closed position.

For historical authenticity, or if you just don't like the look of side-mounted steel slides, go for either undermounted steel slides or wood slides, which glide in wood slots in the drawer sides. Undermounted drawer slides are expensive, especially full-extension models. While they take up some of the available drawer depth, they do allow for a slightly wider drawer. Since they're less exposed than side-mounted slides, they will stay cleaner than side-mounted slides.

▲ THIS NARROW, CUSTOM-DESIGNED DRAWER keeps cooking oils standing up straight in the front while hot pads and mitts stack up behind.

◄ LARGE POT DRAWERS LIKE THESE require sturdy drawer slides, and side-mounted slides are generally more efficient than bottom-mounted slides. It's critical to specify full-extension slides for pot drawers to make all items easy to access.

Drawers versus Pull-Outs

DRAWERS ARE BIG THESE DAYS, **both in status and in size. Drawers have always been the ideal storage** containers for cutlery, paper goods, utensils, linens, spices, and odds and ends, and they are gaining popularity as vessels for pots, pans, and cooking ingredients, such as oils and vinegars, as well.

But there's still a case to be made for cabinets with doors and pull-out shelves. Some cooks like pull-out shelves because they can hold a range of objects, and since the edges of a pull-out shelf are just 2 in. to 4 in. high, stuff can't be overstacked, so everything is accessible. On the other hand, you have to open the door, then pull out the shelf—unlike a drawer, which takes a single operation to access the contents.

◤TALL CABINETS SUIT THE TALL COOK WHO WORKS HERE, and the large pot drawers are pretty handy, too.

◀THESE HANDSOME PULL-OUT SHELVES are made of ⅝-in. dovetailed maple. The shelves are adjustable to suit the heights of a variety of contents.

◀THESE DEEP DRAWERS HANDLE THE FAMILY'S DAILY DISHES and are easy to reach from the dishwasher and easy to access from the dining room.

Hinges

THE VAST MAJORITY OF CABINET DOORS SWING, much to the delight of kids of all ages, who invariably swing—and lean—as they survey cabinet contents for good stuff. The European cabinet revolution in the 1950s that brought us frameless cabinets also brought the concealed cup hinge, a complicated-looking hinge that allows a cabinet door to be easily adjusted, both during installation and years later, when a door might have sagged. These days, concealed adjustable hinges are also available for face-frame cabinets. Larger concealed hinges may require a mounting block on the inside of the face frame. A more expensive but cleaner detail is to run the mounting block the full vertical length of the inside of the face frame.

Despite the ease of installation and operation of concealed cup hinges, butt hinges are a traditional favorite for inset doors and are a less obtrusive alternative on glass-paneled cabinets, where the hinge is always in view.

As with any system, the most problematic components of a cabinet are the parts that move. That puts hinges at the top of the list (drawer slides are a close second), so don't skimp on quality here. Or bypass hinges altogether and go for that restaurant-kitchen standard, the sliding door.

▲ A STAND MIXER CAN TAKE UP A LOT OF ROOM on a countertop, but it's also a heavy load to haul from a cabinet. Here's a sweat-free solution: Store the mixer on a shelf that rises to the occasion from a base cabinet to countertop height on specialized hardware.

◄ THIS SMALL KITCHEN MAKES USE OF EVERY SPACE, including the angled cabinet, which is ideal for storing flat items, such as pans, trays, and cutting boards. Cabinets are frameless, but the doors are traditional, with maple frames and Honduras mahogany panels.

Finishing Cabinet Tops and Bottoms

A S YOU HOME IN ON YOUR FAVORITE CABINET STYLES, consider how they will fit into the room at top and bottom. Trimming cabinet tops and bottoms contributes more to style and function than it might seem. Cabinets can stop short of the ceiling or go all the way up to be trimmed by crown molding or finished off with a reveal, which is a narrow slot between two surfaces. Cabinet bottoms may incorporate a toespace or, less commonly, may sit on a wide base (cabinetmakers call it a plinth).

While thinking outside (or above and below) the box is easy with custom cabinetry, it's also quite expensive; there's an ever-increasing range of nonstandard cabinets available through stock and semicustom sources that offer interesting details without the sticker shock.

▼ TINY CEILING-HUNG CABINETS MAKE A THREE-DIMENSIONAL frieze around the kitchen. While visually interesting, they don't provide easily accessed storage and should be filled with rarely used items.

◄ RECLAIMED BARN LUMBER—
mostly pine with some hemlock—
was custom sawn to make this
hutch/television cabinet combo
in the dining room. The top of the
cabinets received special attention, with a dark-stained diamond
inlay, crown molding, and a crown
of greenery.

▼ A DETAILED INLAY TRIMS CROWN
MOLDING and the rail over the
microwave to give a distinctive
edge to these cherry face-frame
cabinets. Toespaces are framed
by canted legs. A peek under the
wall cabinets offers a glimpse
at unusual, triangular task-light
fixtures.

► THIS BUILT-IN, FULL-HEIGHT CABINET provides a contrast to its flanking neighbors with a curved top, large pulls, and natural pine finish. Stopping the elaborately trimmed cabinet tops just short of the soffit gives the cabinets more of a furniture look.

▼ THESE CABINETS MEET THE CEILING AND FLOOR in several different ways. Cherry dish cabinets at left abut an overhanging soffit for a sheltered look, while cookware cabinets are flush with the soffit, which continues across the sink with recessed task lighting.

▲ A ROW OF UPPER CABINETS STRETCHES from wall to wall across the tops of the maple wall cabinets. Sandblasted glass is the material of choice in the framed doors and sliding panels.

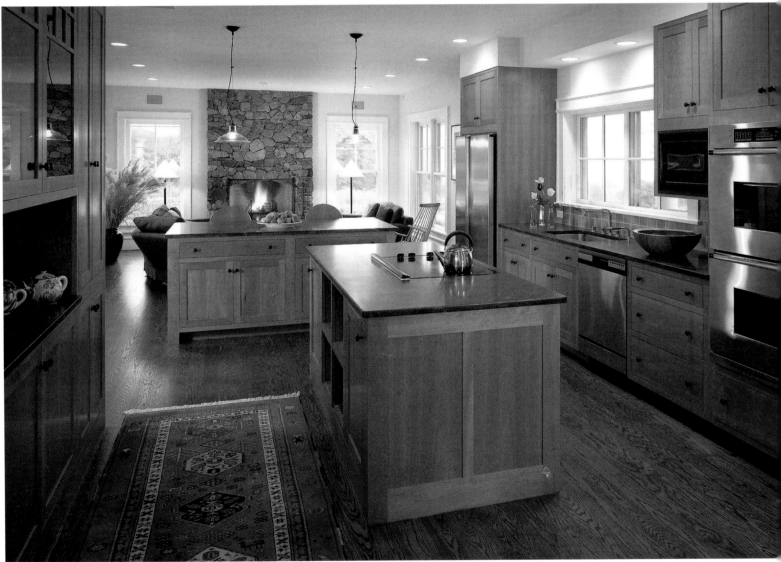

Considering Cabinet Tops

OFTEN, WALL CABINETS DON'T REACH TO AN **8-FT. CEILING**, partly because tall cabinets cost more, and partly because items stored up high are hard to reach. Open cabinet tops are ideal, however, for decorative pottery or baskets, little-used kitchen tools, plants, a painted frieze, or windows—natural light that enters a room from a high window provides the most desirable light year-round, and it bounces off the ceiling to multiply the effect.

Cabinets can also meet a lowered drywall or wood-trimmed soffit that contains lighting and ductwork. For a more traditional look, cover a flush-fitting lowered soffit with a super-deep crown molding to tie the cabinetry visually to the ceiling. If household members are prone to allergy or asthma, consider taking the cabinets to the ceiling or to a lowered soffit to avoid surfaces that collect dust.

Cabinets that reach the ceiling or a soffit often require trimming to hide the joint. An elaborate molding can make the cabinet look more like furniture. Another option is to make a narrow slot (called a reveal) between the cabinet and the soffit or ceiling.

▲ THESE NATURALLY FINISHED CABINETS RECEIVE a jolt of brightness from the white trim. Ceiling-hung cabinets over the island display a collection of copperware and provide a buffer between eating and workspace.

Tackling Toespaces

THE TOESPACE (also called a toekick, kickspace, or kick-plate) is made by a separate recessed platform that supports the cabinet. American-made face-frame cabinets and most frameless cabinets have a 4-in.-high, 3-in.-deep toespace. European cabinets often have tall toespaces, from 5 in. to 9 in. high, which many people like for the sense of lightness the look imparts and because it's easier to clean around cabinets without damaging doors and drawers. But a tall toespace means less interior cabinet space, unless the toespace itself is fitted with a drawer or a pull-out skid or step stool (you can configure 4-in.-high toespaces the same way.)

Toespaces can provide a space for heat/air registers and ductwork for a central system, or even for installation of individual toespace heaters. The blowers in toespace heaters can be noisy, however, so research the options carefully.

Toespaces aren't required. The ongoing popularity of the unfitted kitchen, where pieces are designed to look as if they were collected over time, has spawned the cabinet plinth, which is a wide base that supports the cabinet case, as well as cabinet legs, where stiles of the cabinet frame are continued to the floor to make feet with a toespace in the center. Cabinets with no toespaces are hard to stand at, so it's best to increase the overhang of the countertop and be sure your drawers have full-extension guides.

The toespace also acts as a bumper against overzealous mopping and vacuuming. If you opt for no toespace, consider adding at least a 4-in.-tall base trim to your cabinet. This detail can also apply to the sides of a cabinet, where it's not common to have a toespace. Here, a base trim provides a natural paint break or a change of material that allows for easier repairs if the bottom of the cabinet is damaged by man or beast.

FINISHING CABINET BOTTOMS

This is a typical toespace at front with a flat cabinet side and shoe molding on each side.

Extra-tall European toespace trim board usually covers adjustable cabinet legs.

The toespace trim is continued along flat side with trim board.

Cabinet frame continues to the floor to become a leg.

The toespace is on the front and side; the side can be paneled to match the front.

A traditional cabinet with no toespace can sit on a plinth, which can be trimmed simply, as shown, or with elaborate molding.

A corner pilaster provides a visual leg for the cabinet; the curved cabinet bottom disguises the toespace.

When a toespace is not desired, consider recessing the cabinet under the sink; a handsome detail at a farmhouse sink.

Materials and Finishes

THE CHARM OF CABINETS is that they can take on just about any appearance you want, but that versatility is also what keeps us up at night trying to decide which materials and finishes are just right. Most of today's kitchens are natural wood, whether solid or veneered onto the cabinet case, doors, and drawers.

Solid wood and wood veneers, of course, do need finishing. This may be a stain (for color, not protection) that's finished with a protective coating—typically a catalytic conversion varnish applied off-site. Cabinets can also be painted or sprayed with high-gloss polyester finish for a flash of color or high style. Cabinets can also be veneered with metal, plastic laminate, or rigid Thermofoil (RTF). As a rule, stained finishes are easier to touch up than painted finishes; both are easier to repair than Thermofoil, plastic laminate, metal, and high-gloss polyester finishes.

▲ THIS DINING ROOM IS ALMOST ENTIRELY FILLED with cabinets, and the remainder is paneled to match cabinet doors. The lower part of the cabinet has sliding doors, which make good sense because they don't swing into the circulation path.

◀ THESE BUILT-IN CABINETS ARE DESIGNED in the unfitted kitchen style, with various-size pieces, a full-height cupboard, and varying cabinet feet. The more elaborate trim on the cupboard, which features bullnosing, fluted pilasters, an elaborate crown molding, and curved cabinet feet, makes it a focal point.

◀THIS IS NOT YOUR MOTHER'S STOCK CABINETRY, unless she's an artist. These custom-designed and crafted cabinets look like sculpture, but they are really a combination of frame-and-panel doors and flat-slab doors and drawers. Wire pulls are designed with both whimsy and easy access in mind.

▶ COMBINING PAINTED CABINETRY GIVES A KITCHEN an unfitted look, as if pieces were added over time. Here, the freestanding island and china hutch are green, while the built-in cabinetry is natural maple, creating a pleasing visual counterpoint. Porcelain knobs on all cabinetry unify the kitchen.

A Look at Wood

LIGHT, EVEN-GRAINED MAPLE is currently the most popular wood for cabinet doors and drawers; in second place is oak, a traditional favorite that is darker and often highlighted with light flecks, especially quartersawn oak. Cherry, an elegant wood that darkens with time, is in third place, and hickory, pine, and pecan follow, chosen for their comfortable, country look. As a rule, hardwood species age more gracefully than softwoods, which may crack and are softer with wider grain. But using wood as a veneer over plywood, MDF, or particleboard ensures that any species can make the grade as a cabinet surface.

Period kitchens may call for certain species, but bending the rules is allowed. Arts and Crafts kitchens were often quartersawn oak, though cherry is a fine alternative if detailed properly. Douglas fir was common at the turn of the 19th century, and pine and maple were Colonial favorites. Cherry and pine are ideal for Shaker-style cabinets. For a truly authentic period look, ask for hand-applied finishes.

Most cabinetmakers and manufacturers recommend having wood cabinets finished in the factory or shop. This minimizes the shrinking or swelling that can occur when the cabinet moves from shop to residence, allows for better control of the finishes, and permits the use of finishes that can't be safely applied in a residence. Cabinets that are to be painted on site should at least be primed before delivery.

◄ WOOD IS THE CABINET MATERIAL of choice for truly traditional design, but MDF is easy to shape, so you'll see many cabinet details carried out in MDF. This cabinet is wood, however, and mostly solid at that; the beadboard is solid wood, while the cabinet door is veneer-core plywood.

▼ CHERRY FROM FLOOR TO CEILING WITH A NARROW GRANITE interlude makes this a warm and elegant kitchen. These unusual cabinets are a face-frame/frameless hybrid, with the case visible on the sides and top but not the bottom.

HAND-RUBBED FINISHING BRINGS OUT THE NATURAL BEAUTY of wavy cherry in this New Mexico kitchen. Custom-made by a local cabinet-maker, these Shaker-style cabinets are fitted with cherry knobs on lower cabinets and walnut knobs on uppers.

THIS UPPER CABINET IS PART of a new built-in china cabinet. An artist gave the cabinet a "faux-relic" finish with many layers of paint. Panels and frame are solid wood, and panel products are wheat-straw particleboard and a medium-density fiberboard called Medex™, both formaldehyde free.

THIS KITCHEN IS IN A NEIGHBOR-HOOD SURROUNDED BY ORCHARDS, so rampant dust precluded the use of intricate cabinetry with panels and molding. The easy-to-clean choice was rigid Thermofoil (RTF), a heat-formed laminate that wraps around the cabinet parts to form a permanent bond.

What's in a Cabinet Case?

FACE FRAMES, DOOR FRAMES, AND DRAWER FACES are often constructed of solid wood, but cabinet cases rarely are. The sides, bottoms, and tops of a case—whether face-frame or frameless—are commonly built from sheet goods, also called sheet stock, engineered wood, or panel products. Sheet goods are made from wood, wood by-products, and even nonwood sources. The most common are plywood, MDF, and particleboard. All of these materials make cases that are significantly more dimensionally stable than solid wood.

Plywood (the stuff in cabinets is called veneer-cored plywood) is stronger and more water resistant than other panel products, and it holds screws better, weighs less, and is easier to curve—but it also costs more. A new twist on plywood is combined-core plywood, a sandwich of plywood and MDF or particleboard. This panel is smoother than plywood and lighter than MDF.

Many cabinetmakers use MDF or particleboard alone for moderate and low budgets, and some cabinetmakers actually prefer these materials because they are dimensionally stable and provide a smooth face for plastic laminate and wood veneer.

Regardless of what it's made of, a case needs to be finished inside and out with some type of material for both aesthetics and durability. The finish can range from paint to wood veneer to laminates. Here's the lowdown on some of the most common choices: Wood veneers are available in many species; maple and beech are common for the interior of custom-quality cases. Laminates include vinyl and paper films, melamine, and high-pressure plastic laminate. Melamine that is heat-fused onto particleboard makes an ideal interior surface for a cabinet case. It's half the price of hardwood plywood, washable and tough, cheaper than high-pressure laminate, and won't peel—unlike films and foils, which are not water resistant.

▲ THESE CUSTOM CABINETS ARE CONSTRUCTED from solid wood and veneer-core plywood.

◄ CHERRY CABINETRY WOODWORK MESHES SEAMLESSLY, with window trim. Even the chairs are cherry, and the effect is balanced nicely by the cool colors of marble, gray paint, and black appliances.

▶ ANYONE WITH A CHEMICAL SENSI-
TIVITY TO THE OUTGASSING that
can occur with most new wood
cabinets will appreciate metal
cabinets. They needn't be the
garden variety, as evidenced here
by these sleek, high-gloss lemon-
yellow numbers.

▽ A WHEAT-COLORED KITCHEN
TAKES ITS WARMTH and texture
from beadboard panels in inset
framed doors, as well as from the
textures found in the wallpaper,
tile backsplash, and curtains.

◄ WHITE-PAINTED WOOD CABINETS
ARE COVERED with metal-framed
translucent glass to give the cabinets a soft, ethereal look. Interior
shelves are glass.

Glass Doors

GLASS IS A FAVORITE DOOR PANEL **for wall cabinets that store glassware and dishes, but glass doors cost two to three times as much as solid doors. It's possible to save money by ordering cabinets "prepared for glass" and have glass supplied locally, even from a shower-door supplier. Clear-glass cabinets require a finer finish on cabinet interiors than textured-glass doors.**

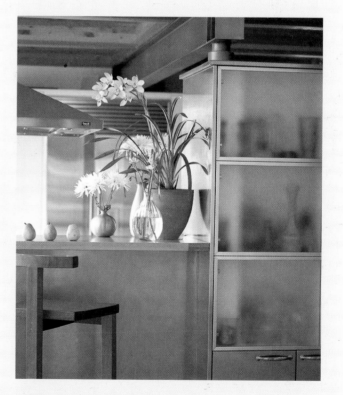

▲ STEEL AND WOOD COEXIST PEACEFULLY IN THIS AIRY, elegant kitchen. Cabinets are stainless steel with translucent glass panels above and solid doors below. The carefully chosen contents add abstract color to the kitchen.

▲ NATURAL MAPLE AND YELLOW-PAINTED FRAMELESS CABINETS make a sunny galley kitchen. Stainless-steel appliances, sink, and clock and the exposed steel structure add a cool contrast to the warm colors of cabinetry, backsplash, and floor.

▲ THESE CABINETS ARE CUSTOM
BUILT AND FEATURE BEADBOARD
paneling highlighted with well-
placed lighting that finishes the
inside of the wall cabinets. Pull-
out baskets make casual drawers.

▶ THIS IS A CONTEMPORARY KITCHEN
FROM FLOOR TO CEILING, from the
matte tile laid diagonally to the
single-pane windows. Cabinets
have flush joints, smooth surfaces,
and metal details.

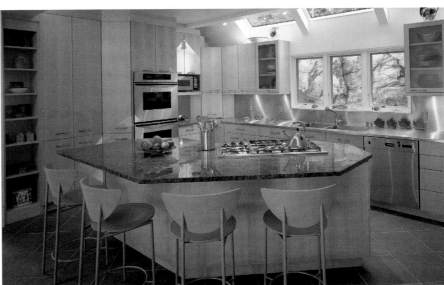

Cabinet Accessories

THE DOORS AND DRAWERS ON A CABINET may grab attention for their aesthetic pizzazz, but what keeps attention in a kitchen is how well the cabinets are fitted to work efficiently. Hardworking accessories, from appliance garages to lazy Susans, should be designed to suit a cook's work method, storage needs, and budget.

Cabinet accessories worth consideration include slide-out and pull-out shelves, vertical slots for trays and baking sheets, good-size spice drawers, and small-item racks that fit on the inside of cabinet doors. Most households would also benefit from cabinet accessories geared toward recycling, such as pull-out twin trash receptacles and undercabinet bins for compost. Many of these accessories are available as aftermarket products, but building them in makes for a better-integrated, and frequently more durable, accessory.

▲ A CUSTOM-MADE DRAWER is fitted with a maple insert for sorting cutlery. Full-extension drawer slides allow for easy access to the back compartments.

◄ THERE'S A PLACE FOR EVERYTHING IN THIS PINE HUTCH, which features closed-door storage above, along with an open dish rack and drawers fitted with cutlery slots below. Custom cabinetry details include dovetailed corners on the drawer box and rounded top edges on the drawer sides. The bead on the edge of the cabinet face frame is integral, not glued or nailed on.

◀ CAKE FLOUR, SUGAR, AND ALL-PURPOSE FLOUR are easy to scoop from this specially designed drawer fitted with Plexiglas boxes that won't leak. Baker's basics like salt, baking powder and soda, vanilla, and frequently used flavorings are kept in the right slot.

▼ THIS DRAWER, POSITIONED AT A BAKING WORKSPACE, has adjustable Plexiglas dividers that keep cake and tart pans aligned and easy to retrieve.

▲ THIS DINING SPACE (AND A KITCHEN NOT IN VIEW) OVERLOOKS the family room in a ski house, so cooks aren't separated from the hubbub, but they aren't bothered, either. A cabinet makes a storage space for dishes and makes a more secure railing than simple metal rails; the green-tinted concrete countertop is backed by a wood backsplash to prevent falling objects.

Storing Spices

▲ THESE CABINETS OPEN UP TO REVEAL MULTILAYERED spice storage right near the professional-style range. Shelves are fixed and spaced to allow various-size spices, and the door shelves have a safety rail. The substantial solid cherry cabinets keep out heat and light when closed, and the active cooks check spices for freshness.

STORING SPICES can make a jumbled mess if not given some forethought, but there's no one cabinet accessory that suits everyone. Here are some things to consider: Light and heat are enemies of spice life, so keep only much-used spices out in the open and near the range; the others need a home in the dark. (Even a cabinet right next to a hardworking stove gets too much heat for long-term storage, though it's fine for spices that see frequent use and replacement.)

Some cooks like the uniformity of same-size jars lined up on a rack built to size, while other cooks collect spice jars and tins of all types and sizes. A drawer with slanted shelves or racks allows for a slight variation in jar size, while a deeper drawer accommodates spice containers of all sizes—though they'll be standing up, so you have to be willing to label the tops.

Accessories tailor-made for spices, such as wall-cabinet lazy Susans, racks that drop down from the bottom of a wall cabinet, and back-of-door shelves, are available not only as built-ins but as aftermarket products. Chapters 3 and 5 offer more spice-storage ideas.

▶ THIS HANDY CABINET NEXT TO THE COOKTOP is filled with slots for pans and baking sheets. The half-height slots keep smaller items from getting lost.

Accessories for Recyclables and Trash

Look for pull-out garbage and recycling bins, slide-out trays for trash cans, composting drawers, and other options for dealing with kitchen waste. It's possible to purchase these accessories after cabinets are in place, but it's much easier to figure in trash as the cabinets are designed. Consider where you prep food and locate the wet garbage can close by, even right under the countertop, so the bin can be pulled out with a foot and the trimmings swept in. The same goes for compost containers. Think in terms of locating recycling bins in a handy but out-of-the-way spot, preferably next to the outside door—a mudroom off the kitchen would be a perfect spot.

▲ IT'S COMMON TO SEE VERTICAL SLOTS BUILT into cabinet interiors, but this kitchen is filled entirely with drawers. To accommodate flat items, a large drawer is fitted with slots.

THIS DRAWER IS THE BRAINCHILD OF A PASTRY CHEF, but it's a model for anyone with a collection of small baking tools. Plexiglas dividers fit into the drawer without requiring any customizing of the drawer itself, so the drawer could be used for other types of kitchen tools if desired.

A MAGNETIC STRIP FIXED IN A DRAWER NEAR THE COOKTOP keeps knives clean, neat, and out of sight while easy to access.

DRAWER DIVIDERS LIKE THESE CAN KEEP cooking tools untangled. Slots to the back are easy to reach when the drawers open completely on full-extension hardware.

Corner Accessories

ONLY THOSE WITH GALLEY KITCHENS—which have no corners—don't have to think about how to fit a base-cabinet corner to make that big, dark space easier to access. Cabinetmakers offer a range of accessories, including lazy Susans and swing-out, pull-out racks. The best lazy Susans are fitted with a high ledge or a curved backing to keep items in place. Remember that the more moving parts, the more expensive the accessory. On wall cabinets the corner is not as tough to access because cabinets aren't as deep. Still, if the corner cabinets are fitted with open shelves and no doors, objects will be easier to access and the kitchen will look more spacious.

▲THE CONTENTS OF THESE CABINET CORNERS are completely accessible with sturdy wire shelves that swing out. Wire shelves keep items visible and allow for air circulation.

▲ONE OF THE SIMPLEST WAYS TO DEAL WITH CORNER cabinets is to fit them with standard doors, as shown here, and run fixed shelves into the corner.

◀ A PANTRY THAT'S CLOSE AT HAND
IS A TIME- AND STEP-SAVER for anyone. Here, a full-height pull-out
cabinet handles that job next to
the refrigerator, keeping storage
situated in one place in the
kitchen of a professional cookbook writer.

3

Open Shelves and Pantries

While cabinets are a kitchen mainstay, providing invaluable closed storage space, open shelving is a useful and visually appealing alternative worth incorporating into any kitchen design. Open shelves are perfect for showing off kitchen treasures and dishware, and they can make retrieving and putting things away fast and simple. On the downside, open shelves allow contents to get dirty or dusty faster, and neatness—or the lack of it—is always on display.

While collections of pottery, cookbooks, and neat stacks of dishes and mugs look charming on open shelves, not everything warrants a look-see, especially when kitchens are open to living areas. Enter the pantry, where kitchen essentials are on display for easy access but safely behind a door when not in use. Pantries don't have to be separate rooms as in days of yore; they can be designed in all sizes, from walk-in to lean-in, pull-out to roll-out, for any kitchen, big or small.

◀ BUILT-IN MAPLE SHELVES ARE THE CORNERSTONE of this bright kitchen, providing display space for decorative pieces as well as space for everyday dishes. Positioning the shelves in front of the window allows the home-owners to have their storage and see through it, too.

Shelves

WHETHER YOU'RE DESIGNING A KITCHEN FROM SCRATCH or just want to spruce things up, shelves offer a lot of bang for the buck in terms of aesthetics and function. An open shelf or two can easily be wedged between wall studs, above a door, or along a stairway.

It's important to match the function of the shelf with the design of the shelf, considering size, method of support, material, and finish. Display decorataive items on shelves that look good, too, such as glass shelves, or painted or stained wood shelves with a wide edge band and curved brackets. Heavy objects—canned goods, stacks of plates, and cast-iron pans—require closely spaced supports and strong shelves, such as plywood. Veneer or paint can make the beefiest shelves look great. Adjustable shelves offer flexibility, while fixed shelves offer a more traditional appearance.

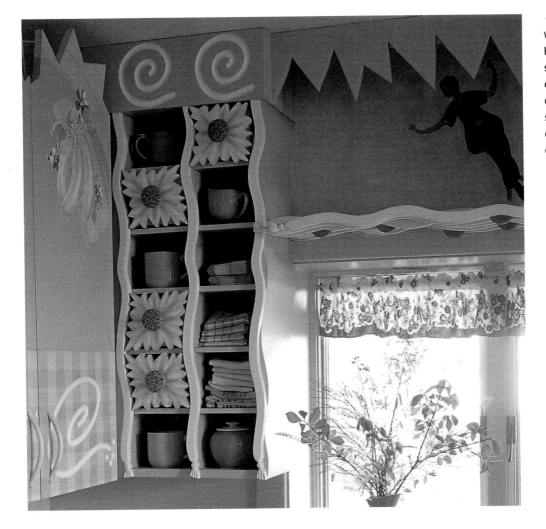

◀ THESE CUBBY-SIZE SHELVES LOOK WAVY, but that's an illusion made by curvy trim applied to the shelf sides. Petal-faced drawers provide contained storage for napkin rings or other loose items, while open shelves create pretty but useful display space and storage for colorful mugs and linens.

▲A SINGLE BAND OF OPEN BOXES AFFORDS sturdy shelf space for storage jars within and baskets above. Boxes are thick, bead-edged, and painted solid wood, and a cleat helps support the upper edge of the shelves.

◄THESE THICK MAPLE SHELVES ARE SUPPORTED on threaded metal rods and hung from the ceiling structure, creating a sleek, elegant system for storing daily dishes and glassware.

Sizing up Open Shelves

SHELVES CAN BE AS NARROW as 2 in. or as wide as 2 ft., but here are some standard guidelines: Allow 8 in. minimum for cookbooks, 8 in. to 15 in. for dishware, and 12 in. to 18 in. or more for large items such as roasting pans, slow cookers, and the like. If you space shelves far apart, you'll be tempted to stack dishes and glasses too high. Better to space more shelves closer together, which makes it safer and easier to access dishes.

Narrow, open shelves from the countertop to just above head height provide easy-to-reach storage. Over a much-used workspace, keep a 12-in.-deep shelf about 30 in. above the countertop, the standard at sinks and cooktops (this is a great spot for undershelf task lighting). Any shelves at your head height and lower should, of course, be shallow, as they can obstruct use of the workspace below.

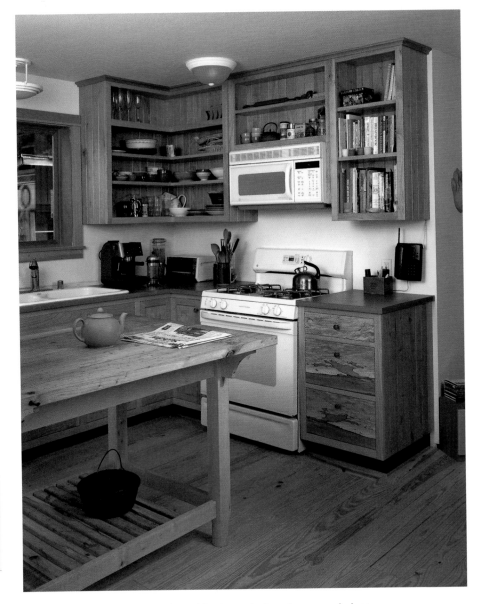

▲ THESE UPPER cabinets are designed as open shelves, with decorative v-groove-board backs. Cases are face-frame and shelves are solid wood; the top shelf on the left has an edge band. The West-coast cabinet-maker used local woods for much of the cabinets, including alder, spalted maple, elm, and cherry.

◀ THIS THICK PRECAST SHELF, tinted green, fills a niche between cabinets to make a handy shelf. Undercabinet lighting spotlights a potted plant, but any decorative object would look good.

◄ ANY CHANGE IN THE PLANE OF A SURFACE can be an opportunity for storage. Here, a granite countertop steps up an inch to store everyday dishes, and the wood countertop provides both a protective roof and an informal space to eat.

▼ TO GIVE THE EFFECT OF A FREE-STANDING HUTCH, a built-in base cabinet is topped with an arch-topped, face-frame cabinet case with fixed shelves. The inside back of the case is finished with beadboard paneling for a traditional look.

Wood Shelves

THE MOST COMMON SHELF MATERIALS are wood and wood-like materials, such as plywood, medium-density fiberboard, and particleboard. All of these materials are widely available in various thicknesses and all are easy to transform with stain or paint. Before storing heavy objects like cookbooks or a stack of plates, you'll want to consider the strength of the shelving material and the support system it requires. After making sure shelves will stay up, consider what finishes you'd like to give them.

Wood and panel products can all be supported by the same methods, but the spacing of supports will depend on the type of material, the thickness of the shelving, and the edge treatment. Solid wood is stiffer than the same-thickness MDF and particleboard, but not as stiff as plywood. Plywood is dimensionally more stable than wood, too, so it is less likely to warp with humidity changes.

All of these materials will be considerably stiffer with an edge band of wood or plywood attached to the front (the edge band acts like a supporting beam; see drawing on the facing page). The traditional way to support shelves—whether solid wood or panel-product shelves—is with a cleat, a solid-wood strip attached to the wall and running the length of the shelf to help prevent widthwise sag. When sturdy shelving is required, brackets can be added at one or more points across the midspace of the shelf; in fact, if brackets are spaced closely enough, there's no need for a cleat.

Panel products can be veneered with wood, and both wood and panel products can be finished with paint, stain, or a clear or tinted varnish or polyurethane. After shelves are freshly painted—gloss or semigloss works best—it's best to wait a while before loading. Wait at least as long as the paint-can label suggests, then lay sheets of waxed paper loosely on the shelves before stocking them. After a week or two, slide out the waxed paper.

▲ THE FIXED, BULLNOSED SHELVES IN THIS WALK-IN PANTRY are supported by cleats on beadboard paneling, and they've been spaced to accommodate items of varying heights. It's easier to scan the pantry quickly when shelves are narrow. A ribbed-glass door blurs contents (good for those messy days).

To add considerable stiffness to a wood or panel-product shelf, apply a wood or plywood edge band to the front edge.

For strong, basic pantry shelving, install metal standards and support shelves on metal brackets. Recess standards into the wall for a cleaner look.

A thick shelf acquires strength but not weight by being built like hollow-core doors. For a modern look, attach by supporting from ceiling or by using invisible support system.

Brackets are essential for longer spans carrying heavy loads. Notch brackets to receive cleat. Shelf can be removable.

Supporting a shelf on a continuous wood or plywood cleat doubles the distance a shelf can span.

Shelf can slide into dadoes cut into wood boards at sides; for extra support, provide a dado along the back, too.

For a contemporary look, pin or bar supports can be hidden within the shelf and attached to studs.

An L-shaped metal shelf is inset into studs before drywall is installed.

Shelf pins in drilled holes provide support for short-span shelves in recessed walls or in cabinet cases.

Shelf can fit within frame of cabinet case

OR

Shelf can extend past frameless case or wall for more prominence.

▶ THIS ISLAND IS HOME TO A GRID OF FIXED SHELVES of naturally finished solid maple set in a cream-colored stained case. It provides ideal storage for dishes, which can be quickly grabbed and plated at mealtime.

Adjustable or Fixed Shelves?

MAKING SHELVES IN CABINETRY **fixed or adjustable affects how they look and how well they work. Adjustable shelves can be handy for growing families or changing buying habits, especially in a pantry. European-style frameless cabinet cases have adjustable shelves, which can be adjusted by 32-mm increments by moving support pins up or down; the same system can be used for face-frame cabinetry. Adjustable shelves can get quite a workout during the setup phase, and the move from storing baby-food jars to storing packages of Ramen noodles may come sooner than you think.**

For showcasing decorative objects, fixed shelves seem more purposeful, even architecturally noteworthy themselves (and there won't be 32-mm on-center holes up the sides). A period kitchen requires fixed open shelving for authenticity.

▶ EVERYDAY DISHES AND ART CERAMICS PROVIDE a visual focus in this nicely proportioned fixed shelving, which separates a large dining/living space from the kitchen.

◄WIDE SHELVES that are spaced close together make the ideal storage system for linens. These shelves pull out to make it easier to put away tablecloths and placemats, which are too floppy and large to slide easily into fixed shelves.

▼ANGLED STEEL BRACKETS ATTACHED TO THE SIDES of this mobile island hold baking sheets, which then act as shelves that hold smaller flat items. During a major baking session the cart can be turned into a cooling rack as well.

▲SHELVES CAN BE DESIGNED FOR SPECIFIC TASKS, such as storing a collection of much-loved and often-used rolling pins as shown here. The back lip of each channeled shelf allows easy attachment and the front lip holds in the rolling pin.

Glass Shelves

Glass shelves make bright and elegant open shelving, especially to show off glassware and fine dishware. A boon in perpetually overcast climates or in rooms without a lot of windows, glass allows light to bounce around. Glass type and thickness should be taken into account before specific shelving is chosen; here are a few hints.

The edges of a glass shelf figure prominently in its overall look, so edge treatment and glass type should be carefully considered. Standard clear glass actually has a greenish tinge, which is especially apparent at the edge, so if you prefer a clearer glass, look for low-iron Starfire glass.

Glass shelves can be strong, but they have limits. A shelf with a light load and short span can be ⅜ in. thick, but longer spans and heavier loads require a thickness of ½ in. or more, plus intermediate supports. A glass fabricator or cabinetmaker can recommend the appropriate thickness for your particular needs.

▲ RATHER THAN FITTING THIS SPACE NEXT TO A WINDOW with a closed cabinet, the architect designed short-span glass shelves, which allow light to bounce around and highlight decorative dishware. Glass is supported on stainless posts made in a local metal shop and set into angled solid-maple brackets, which in turn are affixed to maple-plywood backsplash panels.

Pantries

T HE PANTRY ADDS MUCH NEEDED STORAGE to today's kitchens. Buying in bulk has breathed new life into the pantry, as has the boom in multiethnic cooking, which requires more shelf space for new ingredients and specialized kitchen tools. Thankfully, a pantry can be fit into most kitchens, whether as a 3-in. shelf between studs or as a walk-in version.

Retrofit a broom closet with U-shaped narrow shelves or reconfigure cabinetry to include a base-cabinet or floor-to-ceiling manufactured pull-out pantry (make sure the pull-out hardware can handle a heavily loaded 6-ft.-tall unit). A step-in pantry can fit in the same amount of storage for a smaller price tag. The walk-in pantry is the queen of pantries, especially if a stretch of countertop can perform double duty as a workspace or temporary bar.

▼ THIS HISTORIC WALK-IN PANTRY IN A large farmhouse in Vermont is an example of how handsome and functional a dish pantry can be. Base cabinets are fitted with both closed shelving for larger pieces and drawers for silverware and linens. Shelves are supported on cleats and corner posts.

Sizing up Pantry Shelves

Pantry shelves should be deep enough **to hold one to four items front to back, but shallow enough to see contents easily. Go for 4 in. to 8 in. for cans, 8 in. to 10 in. for cookbooks, 12 in. for cereal boxes, and deeper for really big stuff, such as bulk bags of dog food.**

Take a cue from grocery stores and stack items front to back first, then side-to-side. Not all the pantry has to be at grab-and-go height; take shelves all the way to the ceiling for storing light-weight bulk items, such as paper towels and picnic baskets, and keep a stepstool handy.

▲ NARROW, ADJUSTABLE SHELVES, WHICH OFFER easily accessed storage, line a small walk-in pantry, also home to the microwave. A pocket door is a space-saving choice in this tight corner.

▶ SHALLOW BUILT-IN PANTRY SHELVES WITH GUARDRAILS make good use of this space alongside the stair between the lower level and the kitchen.

▲ THIS PANTRY, SITUATED OFF THE BACK DOOR OF THE HOME, works as a drop-off spot for groceries and makes putting dry goods away a breeze. Shallow adjustable shelves on the back wall are a practical two-cans deep, while 2-ft.-wide cabinets and shelves at right handle dishes and larger objects.

◀ WHY HIDE DISHES IN CABINETS WHEN YOU can show them off? This eclectic collection is a centerpiece at a major intersection between kitchen, dining room, and living room. The refinished doors were salvaged from an old house and fitted with simple inset ring pulls and no latches.

▲ THE CABINETS IN THIS CHEERFUL PANTRY have the same Shaker-style doors as the kitchen cabinets but are maple instead of cherry. Continuing in a lighter tone, the countertop is white solid surface and the adjustable shelves are painted white.

▶ THIS WALK-IN PANTRY IS FITTED WITH FACE-FRAME cases and fixed shelves supported on cleats and strengthened by a corner post. The traditional design of wide-base cabinets provides potential workspace.

◀ THIS PANTRY PROVIDES STORAGE SPACE FOR DISHWARE, cookware, and baking tools; a microwave is squeezed in, too, for occasional menial tasks, such as defrosting.

▲ ▶ THESE SIDE-BY-SIDE PANTRIES ARE FITTED with the same type of shelves and support systems, but the shelves are configured and spaced in different ways. All shelves are $1/2$-in. plywood faced with a $1\frac{1}{4}$-in. edge band and laminated with melamine to make a tough surface. Support is provided by metal brackets that can be adjusted along metal standards attached to the wall. A U-shaped configuration works well with smaller items, whether dishes or jars, and deeper, straight shelves handle large serving pieces.

Butler's Pantries

THE BUTLER'S PANTRY is a traditional room that has seen a rebirth, even though butlers are largely extinct. Positioned between the dining room and the strictly utilitarian kitchen, the butler's pantry acted as a transition between the formal public space and the working space. Cabinets were nicely finished for storing dishes, glassware, cutlery, and linens, and a sink was provided for washing dishes and glassware. Today's butler's pantry offers the same transition and space for storing dishware, and gives the cook some respite from interlopers, especially if the space is fitted with a small refrigerator and a bar.

▲ THIS BUTLER'S PANTRY ALSO PROVIDES a cozy workspace for baking, with a niche for a mixer and a lowered counter perfect for making pastry and kneading dough.

◀ THIS BUTLER'S PANTRY FIT FOR COMPANY offers both closed and open storage for the family dishes, including thick plate rails wide enough to hold serving pieces. The stainless-steel countertop with integral sink caps a dishwasher, cabinets, and an undercabinet refrigerator designated for beverages.

▲THIS PULL-OUT PANTRY BUILT
INTO CUSTOM CABINETRY requires
sturdy hardware to carry the load
of canned goods and other heavy
food items. Because shelves are
narrow, this pantry allows for
quick and easy retrieval.

◄THIS FORMER CHINA closet finds
a new life as a wine cellar. Simple
plywood cases are fitted with
slide-out shelves. The room, kept
cool year-round, also serves as
storage space for soft drinks,
chocolate, and cold storage when
party preparations are underway.

4

Countertops and Sinks

I t's fair to say that the countertop is like the carpenter's workbench: It's where we lay out supplies, peel and chop, roll and knead, mix and serve. It needs to be tough, level, smooth, and large enough for the work we do. It's not enough to be big, tough, and versatile, however; countertops have to look good, too. But the choices are dizzying, not only for countertop material but also for finish and edge treatments, connections to sinks, and connections to backsplashes. Today, a good answer is multiple choice, and selecting different countertop materials to suit different tasks is frequently the answer.

Choosing a countertop is best done when choosing a sink so the two function, visually and practically, in concert with one another. It may not be a showstopper like a range, but a sink is the hardest-working item in a kitchen, so you won't regret spending a little more for a sturdy, big-enough, good-looking sink—or two. It's not surprising that two-thirds of new kitchens have a second sink—it's a great way to preserve kitchen harmony.

◄ GENEROUS COUNTERTOPS AND TWO SINKS make this a comfortable kitchen for a family. Each sink has a tall gooseneck faucet that makes it easy to fill big pots. The granite countertop overhangs just enough to invite sitting on bar stools, the perfect spot for homework, conversation, or an informal meal.

Countertops and Backsplashes

SUFFICIENT, COMFORTABLE COUNTER SPACE is crucial in the kitchen. The accompanying backsplash serves many purposes, from visual interest, to wall protection, to easing cleanup. The materials chosen for both should be carefully considered on all fronts, from budget, to durability, to looks.

A kitchen needs at least one 36-in. continuous countertop, preferably sink-side. For two cooks, double that, but keep the workspaces separate if possible. Refrigerators and cooktops need landing spaces (15 in. or more if possible) on one or two sides.

Countertop height should be dictated by preference and the purpose the surface will serve. While the standard is 36 in., a countertop used for cutting should be from 4 in. to 6 in. below your bent elbow. Kneading bread and rolling pastry are easier on lower surfaces, while dining countertops can range from table height (29 in. to 30 in.) to 42 in.

▼ BACKSPLASH HEIGHTS SHOULD BE VARIED to suit the needs of a particular area. This granite backsplash stops just under the windowsill, which is a little higher than usual to avoid water damage. For the rest of the backsplash area, the wall is finished with beadboard, a hardier surface than painted gypsum board.

▲ COUNTERTOP HEIGHTS IN THIS
KITCHEN vary to suit the task,
with a 42-in.-high countertop
anchoring the end of a U-shaped
configuration of maple cabinets.
The cantilevered stone counter
with eased edges gets necessary
support from wood brackets.

◄ THESE SPANISH TILES, CALLED
NIMES TACO, are patterned after
Indian fabric designs. They are
commonly used as accent
tiles, but here they make a rich
patchwork backsplash behind a
professional-style range.

▶ UNCOMMON COUNTERTOP MATERIALS ARE THE HALLMARK in this handsome kitchen. In the foreground is a 3-in.-thick teak countertop with eased edges. Countertops at the cooktop and side cabinets are Durango lime-stone, finished with a sealer. Side-counter backsplashes are the same Durango with inlaid squares of mother-of-pearl in alternating colors.

▼ PAINTED BEADBOARD PROVIDES THE PRIMARY BACKSPLASH material in this kitchen, but at the range tile makes a handsome heat- and moisture-proof backsplash. The saying on the hood, "Who art thou with footsteps rude/that darst within my cell intrude," is the coda of a hardworking solo cook.

◄ A MEDLEY OF COUNTERTOP MATERIALS AND TEXTURES harmonize in this handsome family kitchen. Honed slate makes an elegant countertop, backsplash, and aproned sink, while polished granite covers the island—except for a good-size chunk carved out to fit a lowered end-grain butcherblock.

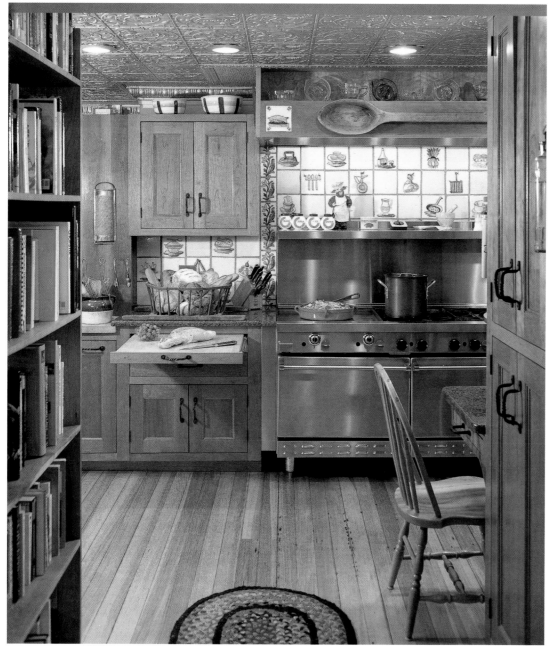

◄ HAND-PAINTED TILES MAKE A HEAT-PROOF AND decorative backsplash alongside and above the professional range in this kitchen that's home to cookbook authors. A wooden pull-out cutting board provides space for slicing and dicing, saving the granite countertops for other tasks.

▶ A CHANNEL WAS CARVED INTO THIS GRANITE COUNTERTOP for the sole purpose of holding eggs—a clever detail designed by the owner, who is a professional cookbook writer and baker.

▼ TO KEEP KNIVES CLOSE TO THE CUTTING BOARD yet safely out of reach, a slot was cut out of this granite countertop to accommodate a plastic box fitted with a wood cap. The wood cap contains slots fitted to the various sizes of blades, and the box can be removed to empty any crumbs.

PLASTIC LAMINATE & SOLID-SURFACING

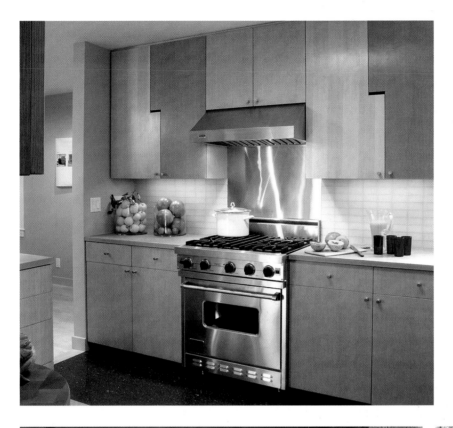

◄ LIGHT COLORS BRIGHTEN AN URBAN San Francisco kitchen with no windows. Light, square-edged solid-surface countertops and rectangular, sandblasted-glass tiles make a cool contrast to the warmer colors of Sitka spruce and Douglas fir cabinets.

▼ A HOUSE IN THE NORTHWEST WITH A DESIGN based on national parks vernacular uses less-expensive modern materials that are in sympathy with native stone and wood. The countertops are solid-surface in a neutral stone color. A second-level countertop conceals lighting and dish storage on the cooking side.

PLASTIC-LAMINATE COUNTERTOPS & BACKSPLASHES

A factory backsplash is inexpensive and makes a watertight connection to the countertop.

The brown line seen in a plastic-laminate self-edge will be hardly visible if laminate is dark and patterned, like this. Solid-core laminate has no dark core but is more expensive and brittle.

A bevel-edge plastic-laminate molding in the same or contrasting color is glued to the countertop edge so that no dark lines show.

A wood or metal edge trim and a backsplash of a different material can give plastic laminate the look of a more expensive countertop material.

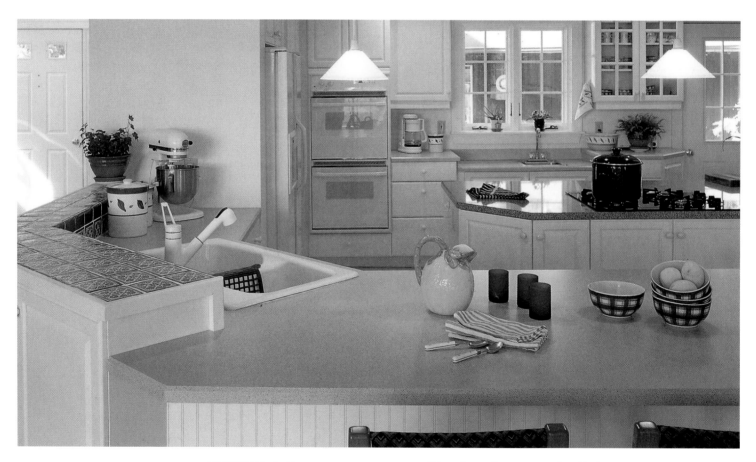

▲ THERE'S NO REASON TO STICK WITH JUST one solid-surface color or texture in a kitchen. Perimeter cabinets are topped with a light gray solid-surface with a stonelike pattern. For accent, the island countertop is topped with a dark gray pattern.

THE COUNTERTOP ALONG THE WALL IN THIS COMFORTABLE kitchen is plastic laminate with a bullnosed wood nosing and wood trim at the bottom of the tile backsplash. The island is solid-surface with enough overhang to make standing at the counter easy.

Plastic Laminate

PLASTIC LAMINATE may not be the latest rage, but it's still used in most kitchens for the same reasons that it surged to prominence in the mid-20th century: It is easy to install, is easy to clean, has good stain resistance, and is economical. The downside? Plastic laminate is not impervious to stains, can't be cut on without damage, can't be repaired, and scorches easily, though high-wear, extra thick, fire-retardant plastic laminate is available for more money. Also, while plastic laminate itself resists water, if water gets into a seam it can damage the substrate, so it's imperative to seal the sink cutout and all other joints.

One aesthetic drawback to plastic laminate—the dark line of the Kraft-paper core visible along a square edge— can easily be covered by an edge band of wood or metal or by beveling the plastic laminate. If you want a more interesting look, digital printing now allows laminate to mimic stone, wood, and other materials with great accuracy.

THIS PLASTIC-LAMINATE COUNTERTOP HAS BEEN ENHANCED with wood trim and is inset with a wood knife holder, which keeps knives safe but at hand near the cooktop.

Solid-Surfacing

A LITTLE OVER 35 YEARS OLD, solid-surfacing is made from polyester or acrylic resin in addition to a mineral filler. Its homogenous quality allows minor scratches to be sanded away, and it is nonporous, easy to clean, highly stain resistant, and can be formed with integral sinks and backsplashes. Solid-surfacing edges can take just about any profile, and it can be formed with color accents at edges or anywhere else on the surface.

Drawbacks to solid-surfacing are its high relative cost (it can cost 10 times as much as plastic laminate and as much as some stones) and its vulnerability to heat—don't set a hot pot directly on solid-surfacing, as there's a slight possibility it can melt or crack.

▲ A WHITE SOLID-SURFACE COUNTERTOP WITH EASED EDGES brightens an urban kitchen that has only one window. Flat white 4-in.-square tile makes a water- and heatproof backsplash. The space is between the cabinets is filled with flat trim topped with crown molding and painted a darker gold to match the softwood floor.

◀ BULLNOSED SOLID-SURFACE MAKES A DURABLE, easy-to-clean countertop for one L of a big kitchen island. This countertop provides food prep and buffet space that serves the bilevel wood-topped leg of the island.

SOLID-SURFACE COUNTERTOPS & BACKSPLASHES

Solid-surface countertop edges can be shaped to many profiles or can be given wood or metal trim.

A square edge with slightly eased corners is a standard profile for a single thickness.

A single thickness can be shaped with a bullnose, bevel, or more complex profile, such as this ogee edge.

An integral backsplash can be fabricated with the countertop.

A solid-surface backsplash can also be a separate piece. Here, bullnosed wood trim makes a narrow shelf for spices.

Solid surfacing can be doubled at the edge for a beefier look. This profile is beveled top and bottom.

This double-layer edge has an ogee on top and a Dupont profile on the bottom layer.

Stripes of contrasting colors or more complex patterns can be inlaid in the shop.

This edge is doubled and given a bullnose profile.

WOOD

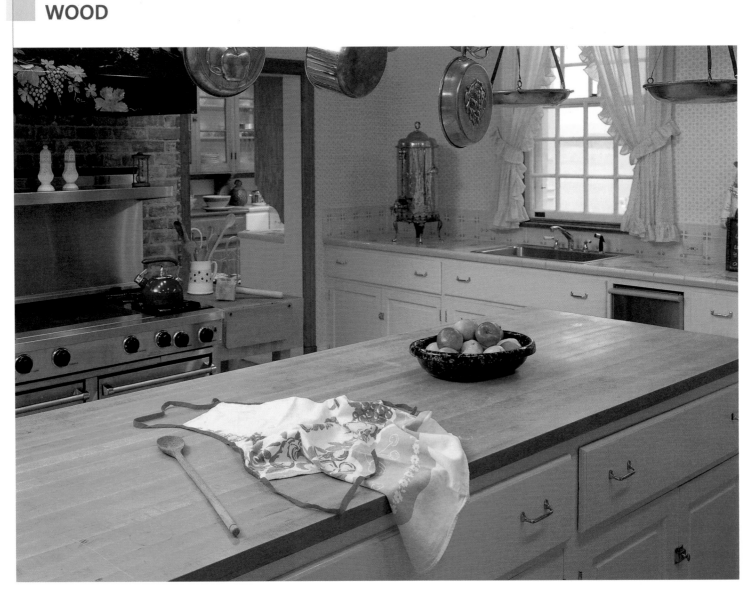

▲ THIS ISLAND IS WELL-USED EDGE-GRAINED BUTCHER BLOCK, while a traditional end-grain chopping block by the range looks beefy but has taken on a more subordinate role as a landing place for hot pots and a place to store tools.

▶ THESE WOOD COUNTERTOPS ARE FACE-GRAIN— not for cutting on— so they received several coats of polyurethane. For looks and water resistance, the soapstone sink is lowered and surrounded by a soapstone rim and backsplash.

A RUSTIC RETREAT ON THE ST. LAWRENCE RIVER has a kitchen island with enough workspace for the whole family. All countertops are thick edge-grained wood with eased edges for comfortable leaning. The big farmhouse-style sink with grooved drainboard is soapstone.

WOOD COUNTERTOPS

Traditional butcher block has end grain exposed. This makes a strong surface for chopping but is porous.

Butcher block with edge grain exposed makes a surface that is less porous and not quite as tough as end-grain butcher block. Hard maple is commonly used for its strength and dense grain.

Nosings can be square (also called flat), square with eased edges, radiused, bullnosed, or given profiles like more complex wood trim.

Face-grain (also called board or plank) countertops are not strong enough to be used for chopping but make handsome surfaces for other uses.

The Beauty and Bane of Wood

WOOD OF MANY SPECIES can work beautifully as a countertop material if it is properly finished and maintained. In addition to its visual warmth and soft sound, it's easy on dishes and glassware and can be shaped into many profiles and configurations; on the downside, it's susceptible to water damage and scarring and costs around twice as much as plastic laminate. Choosing the proper type of wood countertop and finish will help ensure both aesthetic appeal and longevity.

Butcher block is one of the most common types of wood countertops, but the term "butcher block" has more than one meaning. It traditionally refers to end-grain butcher block, which is porous and thus considered unsanitary for restaurant work (but you may feel otherwise, considering some recent studies indicating that wood cutting boards may retain less bacteria than plastic). Today, residential butcher block refers to 1½-in. hard-maple strips laminated together with edge grain up. Edge-grain butcher block is less porous than end grain but not as hard, so while you can cut on it, it'll splinter more than end grain.

Face-grain wood (wider boards) is too soft for cutting but makes a handsome serving or eating countertop. Many species, such as cherry, teak, or oak, can be used for this type of countertop, since you won't be cutting on it.

Your happiness with a wood countertop depends both on a love for the patina it will develop and on diligent maintenance. Sand out scratches or consider them part of the character. A wood countertop used for chopping fruits and vegetables (cut meats only on portable, washable cutting boards) can be left unsealed and maintained with periodic rubdowns with mineral, tung, linseed, or other nontoxic oil.

Wood's Achilles heel is susceptibility to water damage. Rather than air drying wood countertops, dry them thoroughly with dish or paper towels. Wood that won't be used for cutting can be sealed with countertop-friendly polyurethane (undersides, too, to prevent warping), and any wood countertop around a sink requires several coats on all surfaces.

◀ IN THIS WARM-COLORED KITCHEN ALL COUNTERTOPS are edge-grain butcherblock. To continue the theme of warm tones, the range hood, towels, faucets, hammered bar sink, and light fixtures are all copper or brass. In contrast, an immense, bright-white ceramic farmhouse sink is the centerpiece.

METALS

◄ THIS CUSTOM-MADE STAINLESS-STEEL COUNTERTOP has an integral sink and backsplash, with a large bowl for big pots and pans and a smaller bowl for washing vegetables.

METAL COUNTERTOPS & BACKSPLASHES

Stainless steel, zinc, and copper make waterproof countertops, especially if formed with integral backsplashes. Stainless steel is heatproof, while copper and zinc may require protection from very hot pots and pans. Unlike stainless steel, copper and zinc will acquire a patina. Copper is often given an instant patina with heat or chemicals.

Bent integral backsplash

Integral backsplash bends back to make a 4-in. backsplash. Tile or another material can complete the backsplash.

Quilted metal backsplash or metal tiles applied to backing

A 1-in. or thicker square bent edge is a standard nosing.

A marine edge is angled upward to contain spills.

A metal countertop can be bent over the edge of substrate and covered with wood trim.

A bullnosed metal nosing is strong and comfortable to lean against.

Stainless Steel and Other Metals

THE ULTIMATE IN RESISTANCE to water, staining, and heat is, of course, stainless steel, the countertop of choice in restaurants everywhere. It can be shaped and seamed to provide an integral nosing, as well as an integral backsplash and sink. Stainless steel has a long, long life, and after the first few months, when every fingerprint and scratch shows up, it will develop a patina that hides minor scratches.

The strongest stainless-steel countertops are 16 gauge to 14 gauge (the lower the number, the thicker the steel).

Whatever the gauge, a stainless-steel countertop should be set or formed around plywood or medium-density fiberboard (¾ in. is recommended) to add strength and mute the sound.

Other metals making their way into today's kitchens include copper and zinc, although these are softer and more prone to staining, unlike stainless steel. These materials are ideal for a backsplash, which doesn't see the action that a countertop does.

▲ ALL OF THESE COUNTERTOPS ARE STAINLESS STEEL, but they've all received different edge treatments to suit the task. The sink and food-prep countertops have a marine edge, which is both strong and helpful in preventing drips. Around the range the countertop has a square edge. The backsplash helps redirect steam and grease into the center downdraft vent.

◀ ORIGINAL TO AN EARLY-20TH-CENTURY BOSTON HOUSE, this kitchen cabinet has a new stainless-steel countertop, and the cabinet received fresh paint and pulls made from stock molding painted black. Don't look for a dishwasher, as the owner/architect opted for washing dishes by hand.

▼ SQUARE-EDGED COPPER MAKES AN OUT-OF-THE-ORDINARY countertop material that's at home in a traditionally styled kitchen with white tile and a soapstone farmer's sink.

TILE

▲ THESE BRIGHT GLASS TILES MAKE A CHEERFUL, STYLISH BACKSPLASH in a colorful kitchen, while the solid-surface countertop is a calming presence. Wood trim hides the joint between countertop and backsplash.

▶ TILE WITH A METALLIC GLAZE AND UNEVEN TEXTURE makes a decorative backsplash that complements the more traditional crackle-glazed beadboard paneling in this eclectic kitchen.

▲ ▶ THESE SATIN-FINISH, ETCHED-GLASS TILES WERE CHOSEN after the owners ran a test on different glass finishes. They sprayed a nonstick spray to each sample tile, then cleaned it with glass cleaner to see if there was streaking or residue. They found that glossy glass tiles showed more streaks and sandblasted tiles retained residue.

Tile

Tile's GREATEST ASSETS are its looks and flexibility. It can take on practically any shape, color, and size, and just a few tiles can add spice to a kitchen. Tile is also resistant to heat and hence makes a great backsplash behind a cooktop. Glazed tile and glass tile are nonabsorbent, so they resist staining and water (stone tile often needs a sealer to be nonabsorbent).

It is grout that makes tile less than perfect, as grout can stain easily. Stain-resistant additives and color can be incorporated into cement-based grout to improve its performance, or grout can be sealed. Epoxy grout is more expensive than cement-based grout, tends to yellow, and is a bear to work with, but it is harder and more resist to staining and mildew.

Because the joint is the vulnerable part of a tile countertop, it makes sense to go for the narrowest joint possible, but before assuming you can go with hairline joints, consider the regularity of your tile—handmade will be more variable, stone tile more precise. The larger the tile and smaller the joint, the more even the surface will be, a consideration if stemware is set on the counter. In any case, equip a tile countertop with cutting boards.

The cost of tile ranges from economical —for the handy homeowner with discount tile—to expensive, with glass and hand-painted art tile at the peak. Glass tile, the new darling of kitchen design, has a wonderful, luminous look, but if tile is translucent throughout, the setting bed must be perfect.

▲THIS BACKSPLASH IS TUMBLED MARBLE WITH INSET ceramic tiles, each with a charming bas-relief face. Contrasting mosaic stone tile fills and frames the arched recess over the downdraft vent/backsplash. The countertop is honed "Absolute Black" granite with a Dupont profile.

TILE COUNTERTOPS & BACKSPLASHES

Tile countertops can be trimmed with wood or metal, allowing the use of only flat tiles throughout.

Coved tile makes a watertight joint.

A short tile backsplash can be topped with long border tiles or wood trim.

The backsplash is a good location for smaller or art tiles.

V-cap tile nosing contains spills. This joint requires a thick mortar bed.

Top edge tiles have radiused edges.

▲ TO GIVE THE LOOK OF SOLID SLATE WITHOUT THE EXPENSE, slate tiles are laid with a same-color cement grout and finished with a self-edge and slate-tile backsplash.

◄ THE RED, CEMENT-BASED GROUT USED IN THIS KITCHEN not only hides dirt better than white grout but also gives these red tiles a softer, more monolithic look—a handsome contrast to the highly figured granite countertop.

STONE

▼ THIS WESTERN KITCHEN HIGH-LIGHTS ROUGH TEXTURES, from the coarse-edged stone-slab countertops to the tumbled stone-tile backsplash. Cutting boards on such a rough countertop are essential.

▲ THE GRANITE COUNTERTOPS AT LEFT AND ON THE ISLAND HAVE thin, eased nosings and a high-gloss finish, but they still look at home with rough-hewn posts and beams. The surface surrounding the cooktops is honed black granite.

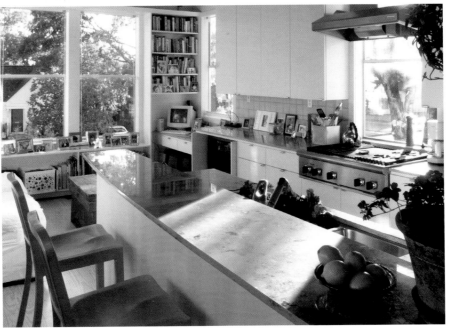

◄ AS A NOD TO TEXAS GEOLOGY, COUNTERTOPS IN THIS Houston house are slab limestone. The raised and curved bar shields kitchen debris from diners. The countertop to the left of the cooktop drops to make a computer niche.

Incorporating Stone in the Kitchen

STONE IS THE GRANDMOTHER OF ALL COUNTERTOP MATERIALS, not only because it's the work surface of the ancients, but because stone is so darn old—hundreds of millions of years old for granite, and a mere million or so for slate. Stone is loved for its solidity, its wide range of colors and figures, and its toughness.

Stone is generally available in two sizes: 2 cm and 3 cm, although you can double up on the edges of a countertop to make it look like 4 cm. Edge profiles for granite and marble range from the almost square with eased edges to bullnosed to highly profiled with an ogee and a Dupont combined (see drawing on p. 102). Just remember that profiled edges are priced by the inch.

Finishes range from rough (recommended only for a backsplash) to honed, which is soft and smooth but not highly reflective, to polished, which is smooth as glass and highly reflective.

Stone may be hard, durable, classy looking, heat resistant, and resistant to scratching, but nothing's perfect, and stone has its bugaboo: Many stones can stain if not sealed properly and regularly. Both the sealer type and the maintenance schedule depend on the stone and your comfort level with how stone can change color over time with use. Just because a stone is soft does not mean it is porous; soapstone is soft but less porous than most types of granite.

Stone is expensive, so it should be accompanied by good service, but it's also popular, so new stone shops are popping up to take your business. Always check recent references. It's best not to buy stone just from looking at a sample, and certainly not from a photo, unless you have absolute trust in the stone vendor; instead, visit the stone yard to view cut slabs up close. Some designers and contractors require their clients to sign off on the slab after seeing it in person. Be aware of where any seams will go and how stones will look when joined. Be flexible about joints and realize that thin stretches of stone—between undermount sinks, for example—are more prone to breakage than wide stretches, and a 3-cm stone slab is less fragile than 2 cm.

If a stone-slab countertop is cost-prohibitive, look for stone tiles, and be sure they are from the same source, as the same-name stone can vary from source to source. Large stone tiles require a sturdy, stiff substrate. Another alternative to solid stone is composite stone (see sidebar on p. 105).

▲ A CENTER ISLAND IS IDEAL FOR A STONE COUNTERTOP, as it's not only a visual centerpiece but it's close to both sink and cooktop. This piece of stone is generous but not so big it needs a seam.

▶ EVEN IF THE SECOND BOWL IS TINY, A TWO-BOWL SINK allows washing dishes and rinsing vegetables to be separated. This stainless-steel sink is under-mounted in a granite countertop, making it easy to sweep water or crumbs into the sink.

STONE COUNTERTOP EDGES

Granite, marble, and limestone slabs are available in thicknesses of 2 cm (about ³/₄ in.) and 3 cm (about 1¹/₄ in.). Soapstone and slate are available in ³/₄-in., 1-in., and 1¹/₄-in. slabs. Thinner slabs require a plywood substrate.

A flat profile with ¹/₁₆-in. eased edges.

A 2-cm slab with profiled wood trim below edge.

A 3-cm slab with a full bullnose.

Dupont profile

Ogee profile

Fillet profile

Ogee profile

Ogee profile

Dupont profile

A 2-cm slab can be doubled just at the edge to give it a beefy look. Seams won't be noticeable if edges are profiled or the lower edge is recessed.

◀ THIS CUSTOM-DESIGNED STAINLESS-STEEL SINK has two layers for two-level food preparation. The granite strip in front of the sink is a separate piece seamed to the countertop on either side; though the sink could be cut from a single piece of granite, the chance of breakage at these fragile joints would be high.

Soapstone and Slate

SOAPSTONE IS EXTREMELY DENSE and won't stain as much as unsealed granite, plus it is softer (it consists of talc, a soft stone, streaked with quartz), so stains can be sanded out. Soapstone darkens from a bluish color to a rich charcoal; you can make that change more uniform throughout a slab or tiles by applying mineral oil periodically. Like slate, soapstone has a more authentic old-house look than granite. It is easily worked and thus can be given edges of various profiles, but a squared, slightly eased edge offers the most traditional look. Soapstone also makes a handsome farmhouse-style sink.

Slate is subtle and soft in appearance, although it can have a visible figure, and it's good at hiding dirt. Like soapstone, it looks at home in any traditional American kitchen, such as Arts and Crafts, Shaker, or Colonial style. Slate is fairly soft as a material and shouldn't be cut on; it can also chip if you drop a heavy object on it, so consider easing the edges for a more resistant nosing design. It's available in black, green, red, gray, and purple. Much slate for countertops needs no sealer—check with the supplier. Slate looks best honed rather than polished, and typically has a square edge with slightly eased corners.

▶ SOAPSTONE IS RELATIVELY SOFT AND CAN BE EASILY CUT and shaped on site, as these countertops were. In keeping with the traditional aspect of the soapstone, Douglas-fir wall cabinets have hand-blown seeded glass, which provides an old-world character.

▶ THIS COZY KITCHEN HAS AN APPEALING TWO-TONE SCHEME, with chunky soapstone countertops atop dark cabinets fitted with black hardware. The soapstone farmhouse sink is for food preparation, while an under-mount stainless-steel sink takes on cleanups.

▼ HONED SLATE MAKES A COOL-TONED BACKSPLASH and countertop material in this kitchen filled with con-trasting warm-toned cabinetry. The piece behind the range has a wilder figure than the backsplash slabs on either side, creating a focal point.

About Composite Materials

OMPOSITE MATERIALS HAVE THE LOOK OF STONE but they are man-made from minerals or stone and polymers (solid-surfacing is a composite, but it has a big enough following to be in its own category). Fiber-cement countertops, such as the well-known Fireslate (one of several types used for lab counters), are strong and resistant to heat but not always resistant to staining, so they must be sealed periodically.

Engineered stone is a new composite countertop material that mixes 90-plus-percent ground-up quartz or granite with a resin binder. These countertops are non-porous, like solid-surface, but heat resistant, scratch resistant, and supremely durable, like solid stone. Many colors and patterns are available and the finish can be polished, honed, or sandblasted. Engineered-stone countertops have the look of stone to a large extent, but expect uniformity in this composite material, unlike solid stone, which often differs from slab to slab.

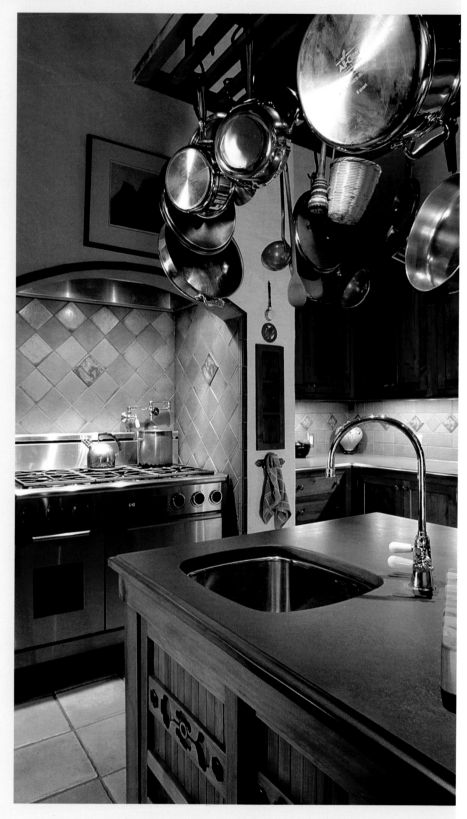

▶ A NEW HOUSE IN NEW MEXICO HAS AN OLD-WORLD CHARM, thanks to a combination of new and old materials. The soft green countertops are Fireslate, a composite stone used in laboratories. To provide stain resistance, they're given a coat of tung oil twice a year. The pot rack is an old gate hung from the ceiling, and the island cabinetry is a Japanese *tansu* chest.

CONCRETE

▲ IN A ROWHOUSE KITCHEN, charcoal-tinted concrete counters were wisely precast after the sink was purchased and measured. The front of the sink was cast with joints to preclude cracks. Periodic waxing reduces the porosity of the countertop.

▶ CONCRETE HAS A LIGHTER SIDE, AS SEEN IN THIS lively family kitchen. Countertops for the raised bar and the base cabinets were precast with a square edge. The warm tint blends with the warm-tone woods, floor, copper pendants, and bright tile accents in the backsplash.

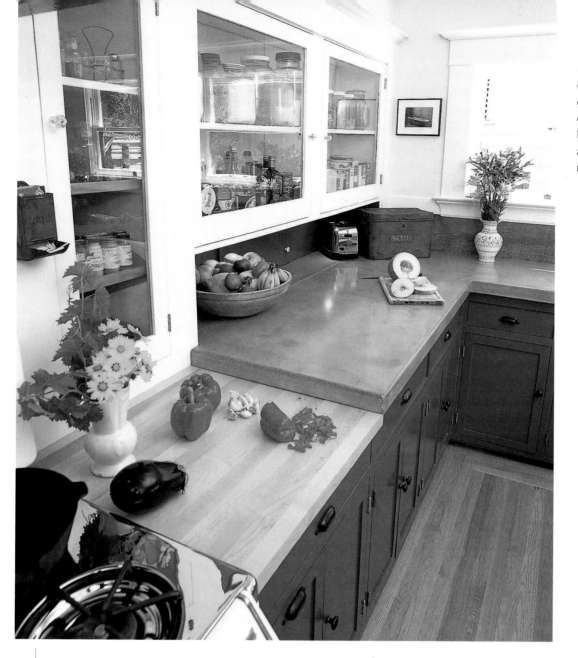

◀ THIS THICK, GREEN-TINTED CON-
CRETE COUNTERTOP WAS PRECAST
on site and lifted into place on
cabinets original to this 1920s
bungalow. Concrete gives way to
a lowered butcherblock counter
next to the restored 1940s range.

The Versatility of Concrete

CONCRETE HAS LONG INTRIGUED DESIGNERS and builders, and recently homeowners have become enamored of this chameleon-like material. Colors are infinite and can be integral or applied, finishes can be glossy, satin, or matte, and edges are just as varied. But this miracle countertop has some caveats. First, concrete must be sealed for food use, either with a topical sealer (better at protecting against stains but vulnerable to scratches and heat) or a penetrating sealer (easy to apply and reapply,

more natural looking, and not damaged by scratches or hot pots, but susceptible to staining or etching by acids).

Second—and more critical—the quality of the finished work is directly related to the skill of the artisans, although an amateur with patience and a love for concrete can make a beautiful countertop. Paradoxically, this makes concrete one of the most accessible and one of the hardest to perfect of all countertop materials. See p. 186 for an excellent resource for making precast concrete countertops.

▲ ▶ THIS CONCRETE COUNTERTOP LOOKS CHUNKY but is in fact only about ½-in. thick across the countertop. Its thickened edge was formed by a 2-in.-diameter PVC pipe ripped into thirds. Unhappy with commercial staining products, the owner/architect rubbed his coffee into the raw concrete, liked it, and applied several additional coats. He sealed the stain with a water-based floor sealer.

CONCRETE COUNTERTOPS

Both cast-in-place and precise concrete must be reinforced with mesh and reinforcing bars. Reinforcing bars and mesh that is closer than 1½-in. from the surface may "ghost" (show through), but epoxy-coated reinforcing may reduce this tendency.

Square concrete edges should be eased slightly to prevent chipping.

If substrate is exposed, cover with a strip of dark plastic laminate or metal (not aluminum).

Concrete can be colored through the body or tinted after placing.

This cantilevered concrete is tapered, both for looks and to reduce mass.

Cabinet cases built from ¾-in. plywood are best for supporting thick concrete countertops.

Concrete countertops require sealing before use; the type of sealer depends on the desired look, the use of the countertop, and the preferred maintenance method. Always use cutting boards.

The Kitchen Sink

DON'T SKIMP ON SINK SIZE, especially not the prime sink in a much-used kitchen. A big sink accommodates big pots and pans, whereas the old standard (two bowls of the same size) doesn't suit heavy-duty cooking. A two-bowl setup with one large sink—big enough for a roasting pan or cookie sheet—and an adjacent 15-in. bowl makes sense if you like to keep a dish drainer in the second bowl rather than on the counter. Consider the divider between a multibowl sink, too. If it's lower than the rim, there's less chance of overflow—not that you would ever leave the faucet running.

Sinks can be mounted under the counter (undermount), integral with the countertop, or drop in (the farmhouse sink, with its exposed apron, is in a class by itself). Drop-in sinks are generally less expensive than undermount sinks, but undermounts have a cleaner look and make it easy to brush crumbs into the sink.

▲ THIS SALVAGED APRON SINK WAS MEANT TO BE UNDERMOUNTED on the sides, but the designer/owner liked the look of the rounded corners so he butted the concrete countertop to the sink. The nickel-plated brass plate for the faucet includes a centered air switch for the garbage disposal.

◄ THIS RECLAIMED CERAMIC SURGEON'S SINK FINDS a new home as a second sink in a new hutch that was built to look old. White subway tiles make a handy ledge. Countertops are soapstone.

Sink Materials

STAINLESS STEEL IS THIS MILLENNIUM'S FAVORITE SINK for good reason. Stainless-steel sinks are easy on dropped dishes and glassware, can handle hot pots, come in many sizes and shapes, and are easy to care for (brushed is a lot easier than shiny). They are also relatively immune to going out of style. The best residential quality stainless is 18 gauge (thicker than 20 gauge) and has an 18/10 content (meaning 18% chromium and 10% nickel). But 20 gauge is perfectly acceptable, especially for a second sink. Look for a sound-dampening undercoating. Stainless-steel sinks aren't necessarily uniform in looks: Some look silvery, some look more subdued, and brushed finishes vary. Stainless steel can be easily scratched, but over time it becomes uniformly scratched, so the fingerprints that drive you crazy at first will diminish over time.

Enameled cast-iron sinks look great and are tough as nails—especially to dropped dishes. A soft rack or cushion at sink bottom and laid across the dividing dam can solve this problem. These sinks are relatively pricey and come in many colors, but white is both timeless and stylish. Most models are self-rimming (undermount models require proper support). Enameled cast-iron sinks are thick, so a bowl will be smaller inside than a stainless-steel sink with the same outside dimensions.

Ceramic sinks are similar to enameled cast iron in looks, but not as strong or resistant to chipping. Hand-painted farmhouse-style ceramic sinks make an artful, if somewhat fragile, statement in a kitchen.

Solid-surface sinks are typically integral with a solid-surface countertop, making a watertight assembly. They

◄ AN ENAMELED CAST-IRON SINK LOOKS RIGHT at home in this bright kitchen. A rubberized pad over the sink's dividing dam makes it less likely for the family scullery crew to break dishes. A pull-out sprayer and easy-to-use looped lever aid in wash-up chores.

▶ A STAINLESS-STEEL BAR SINK FINDS THE PERFECT SITUATION at the edge of this workspace, across from the refrigerator and easily accessed from the informal eating space.

are softer and more prone to staining and scratching than most sinks, but blemishes can also be sanded out. Solid-surface sinks can handle boiling pasta water but not a hot cast-iron pan.

Composite sinks are hardier than solid-surface because they are mostly stone mixed with a little acrylic resin and hence boast the heat-resistant, scratch-resistant qualities of stone. Composite sinks have a leg up on stone sinks, though, because they are not porous.

Stone sinks can look integral (they aren't really integral, as all the parts are glued together rather than molded together) or they can be separate, like a farmhouse-style sink with a front apron. Like a stone countertop, a stone sink will often require a sealer.

▲ TO THE RIGHT OF THE SOAPSTONE SINK, THE COUNTERTOP is grooved to provide a subtle drainboard. The porous soapstone makes a perfect surface for countertop and backsplash around the sink. To make a softer landing for dishes coming out of the two flanking dishwashers, countertops there are wood. The graceful gooseneck faucet is supplemented by a sprayer and a separate tap for hot water.

◀ THIS STAINLESS-STEEL, APRON-STYLE SINK HAS A RAILED RACK for soaps and an extended ledge for holding the faucet, hot water tap, and sprayer.

▶ USING GRANITE FOR COUNTERTOPS AND SINKS LETS the material's pattern take center stage in this kitchen. The countertops overlap the sinks to create visual interest with a shadow and to make the sinks easier to install.

FITTING SINK TO COUNTERTOP

An inexpensive stainless-steel sink clips into place and is trimmed by a separate stainless-steel rim.

A porcelain-enamel cast-iron sink is caulked where it rests on the countertop.

An undermount sink with no reveal (also called a flush reveal) is attached to the bottom of a solid countertop, such as stone, composite material, sealed wood, concrete, or solid surface.

Solid-surface and composite-material countertops can be shop fabricated with integral sinks.

A self-rimming stainless-steel sink clips into the side of any type of countertop.

A porcelain enamel cast-iron sink can be flush mounted into a tile countertop (also called a tile-in sink).

An undermount sink with a reveal is attached to a concrete countertop. The top lip of the sink is visible.

Stainless-steel integral sinks are completely seamless.

◄ SOAPSTONE COUNTERS AND SINK, ARE WARM-LOOKING, durable, and relatively soft, and hence more forgiving to glassware than granite. This custom-made sink is 33 in. by 22 in., with 1 1/4-in. sides and a $1^3/_4$-in. bottom. The drain is offset to allow room for a pull-out waste bin below. The sink's apron is chiseled with a Latin inscription meaning "Hunger, the best seasoning," the nightly answer to kids who say, "I'm starving!"

Faucet Fundamentals

CHOOSE FAUCETS AND SINKS IN TANDEM WITH COUNTERTOPS. If you can't decide between a more expensive sink or a fancy faucet, consider the better sink, as it's a lot easier to put in a new faucet after the fact.

Self-rimming sinks have holes punched or formed into the back ledge for a faucet and accessories, while some undermount sinks have ledges for faucet holes and others require that holes be made in the countertop behind. A faucet can be controlled by separate hot and cold controls (called valves) that are either centerset, with valves and spout clustered over a single hole, or widespread, with valves set 4 in. or 8 in. apart. Some farmhouse sinks require the faucet to be mounted in the backsplash. A faucet can also be controlled by a single lever, which is easier to operate, even by an elbow. Supplemental foot- or knee-operated faucet controllers that work by water pressure can allow you to use water without touching the faucet at all, which is handy when working with raw meat or chicken.

Consider how far the faucet extends over the sink and compare faucet dimensions with those of the sink. A taller or longer faucet can swivel between two or even three bowls, and a tall curved spout allows space for tall pots. A pull-out sprayer can extend the length and height of a faucet by several feet. The newly hip commercial swing spout with a 3-ft. flexible hose can turn any sink into a restaurant scullery, but respect its far-reaching spray.

▲ A HAND-PAINTED FARMHOUSE SINK PROVIDES A FOCUS IN this bright kitchen, while a stainless-steel undermount sink adds prep space. The elegant gooseneck faucet clusters hot, cold, and purified water, while a separate sprayer provides supplemental rinsing power.

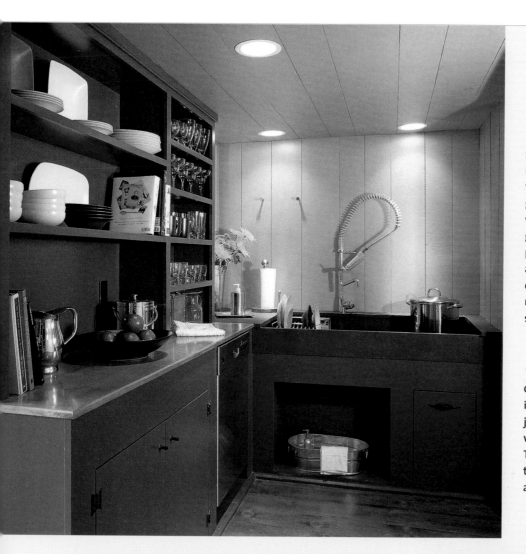

THIS SPACE IS A MODERN SCULLERY NEXT TO THE MAIN KITCHEN area and accessible by the opening visible in the background at the left. A small dishwasher is positioned so that glassware and dishes can be easily put away, and a wood countertop allows for a soft landing for fragile dishes. The commercial faucet makes it fun to wash up in the slate sink.

THE ARCHITECT/HOMEOWNER CHOSE THIS CHICAGO FAUCET for its industrial heft. The double-jointed spout can be positioned wherever it's needed in the sink. The faucet escutcheon affixes to the glass-tile backsplash, making a neat back edge to the sink.

If you opt for a gooseneck faucet or any style without a pull-out sprayer, make sure a hole will be available for a separate sprayer. Likewise, provide holes for any other sink or countertop accessories, such as soap dispensers or purified water or hot water taps that aren't part of the faucet assembly. A water-purification system that has its own tap will be easier to troubleshoot than a system built into the main faucet.

If construction is still going on after fittings have been installed, make it clear that the pull-out sprayer is off-limits for cleaning up: Most pull-out sprayers look like metal but are actually plastic, and paint solvent can damage the surface. If you opt for a brass sprayer, be aware that it can break or chip a ceramic sink if dropped; a soft sink mat and extra caution are helpful here.

▲ THE ARCHITECT/OWNERS OF THIS KITCHEN CHOSE SLATE for both sink and countertop, citing its subtle, soft color and affinity with their Craftsman-style house. A bonus is that they've found this type of slate to be practically maintenance free, as its soft, mottled appearance hides dirt and it does not require sealing.

Dishwashers

I T'S RARE TO FIND A KITCHEN WITHOUT A DISHWASHER **and increasingly common to find a kitchen with two dishwashers. Two dishwashers can take the form of dishwasher drawers stacked or flanking the sink, or two full-size dishwashers flanking the sink or taking up residence at two separate sinks. Most new dishwashers are significantly quieter than older models, but as a rule, money will buy a bit more peace and quiet.**

American dishwashers start at half the price of European models, but many are willing to pay for quieter motors and superior filtering systems. European models (and some high-end American models) continuously filter water so that only clean water is circulated. This takes two pumps, which are quieter than one large pump but need cleaning periodically. As another bonus, two-pump dishwashers tend to have more room for dishes.

Dishwasher tubs are plastic or stainless steel, with stainless tubs costing more but looking good for much longer. More expensive models have stainless-steel arms, while cheaper models use other metals or plastic. Most dishwashers can be fitted with a panel to match (or contrast) cabinetry.

▲ THE DISHWASHER, SINK, AND DISH CABINET make a tight trio in this kitchen, but there's enough space to load and unload the dishwasher comfortably. A wood countertop is gentle on dishes, although most dishes head straight into the glass-door cabinets.

▶ MOST DISHWASHERS SIT DIRECTLY ON THE FLOOR, but if a dishwasher is positioned on a 15-in.-high platform, it's much easier to load and unload. The countertop is, of course, higher than the standard 36 in., but not so high that it can't be used for many kitchen tasks.

From Ranges to Refrigerators

Cooking and cooling appliances are the kitchen equivalent of cars—big machines with lots of style. High performance plays a big part in choosing appliances, along with quiet motors and ease of cleaning. Industrial-style stainless-steel cooking and cooling machines are taking center stage, but close behind are appliances that are almost invisible, like smoothtop cooktops and fridges with integrated panels.

While most of us still make meals in and on our ranges, separate cooktops and wall ovens are gaining momentum, and we've made permanent space for microwaves. Fuel choice depends on availability and cooking preference, with gas cooktops and electric ovens topping the polls for serious cooks. High-heat cooking requires active ventilation to make it easier for everyone to breathe (especially in air-tight houses), to keep moisture and grease from settling, and to prevent cooking odors from lingering.

A refrigerator with well-designed storage and durable parts is essential, because one that's badly configured, noisy, and temperamental will drive you crazy. Today's refrigerators are quieter, full of user-friendly features, and more energy efficient than their predecessors.

◄ PRO-STYLE COOKTOPS DON'T HAVE TO TAKE OVER THE KITCHEN—this one is a standard 30 in. wide. The stainless-steel drawers were designed to fit the space under the cooktop, making it look like a range at first glance, but the ovens are in a wall across the kitchen.

Locating Cooking Appliances

LOCATING COOKTOPS AND OVENS affects how they work and how cooks function. A cooktop against the wall is much better for efficient venting by both hood and downdraft systems, plus you've got a great space to make an artful backsplash. If you do prefer an island cooktop, consider an 8-in. to 10-in. jump in countertop heights to provide a bit of a wall to send smoke and steam to a vent. For built-ins, consider stacking a convection oven, a microwave, and a warming oven all in one wall to consolidate heat.

▼ THIS RANGE LOOKS AS IF IT IS TUCKED INTO AN ALCOVE but it's really an illusion created by the design of the stone hood. Rather than fussing over the fact that the range is deeper than the 2-ft.-deep cabinets, the designer accentuated the range front by applying wood "legs" to the sides.

◄ A STRUCTURAL WALL WAS
REMOVED and a fake beam
added to make a symmetrical
entry to this renovated kitchen.
The cooktop and ventilation hood
take center stage in the new
design. A drop-in cooktop allows
for a big, beautiful tumbled-stone
tile backsplash to incorporate
mosaics. Big drawers below hold
pots and pans.

► COOKTOP AND OVEN ARE NOT
STACKED BUT ARE CLUSTERED
in the cooking workspace of a
kitchen in the Rocky Mountains.
The masonry heater in the corner
energizes a hot plate that can
keep tea kettles and plates warm.

▲ SEPARATE COOKTOP AND WALL OVENS ARE SLEEK
accompaniments to a contemporary kitchen. Going
for wall ovens instead of a range allows ovens to be
positioned at a more comfortable height.

▶ POSITIONING THE RANGE IN AN ALCOVE helps direct
the heat, moisture, and grease from the cooktop and
oven to a range hood, making for more efficient venting. The arched soffit and flanking cabinets make this
range the centerpiece of the kitchen, recalling the
tremendous kitchen fireplaces in old manors.

▶THIS BIG, FABULOUS LA CANCHE TAKES CENTER STAGE in the kitchen of a cookbook author. The range has copious amounts of counter-top space—green-tinted concrete on each side and granite on the 13-ft. island. Cabinets are veneered with micori, an African hardwood.

▲POSITIONING A COOKTOP AGAINST A WALL with plumbing possibilities allows for installation of a pot-filler faucet so that large pots can be filled at the cooktop. If only it were as easy to lug a boiling pot of pasta to the sink.

◀HOW DO YOU PROVIDE COUNTER-TOPS FOR A PROFESSIONAL-STYLE RANGE in a 200-year-old house and still keep that Colonial flavor? Just line the insides of flip-down cabinet doors with stainless steel to make instant countertop land-ing space. The modest, thoroughly unmodern style and proportions of the flanking cabinets tone down the range and keep it from looking flamboyant.

POT RACKS

▶ A PLASTIC-COATED WIRE GRID WITH HOOKS makes a fine pot rack. The black, red, and white tools and pans add color and texture to this bright kitchen.

▼ THERE IS HARDLY A MORE GRATIFYING SIGHT to a cook than beautiful kitchen tools, and these hang from hooks on a stainless-steel pipe. It's tougher to keep them clean if they are hung in the open, but convenience and good looks win out over house-keeping any day.

▲ AN ENTHUSIASTIC HOME COOK DESIGNED her kitchen with the idea that everything had to be easy to access. Her impressive collection of beautiful (and beautifully shined) pots and pans extends the length of the island countertop, where the cooktop reigns.

◄ THIS SIMPLE POT RACK IS MODEST but holds just enough pots and pans for easy access. Pot lids store nicely on pot handles.

Range Options

A RANGE CONSOLIDATES THE HEAT, takes up the least room overall, and costs less than a separate cooktop and wall oven of the same quality. The most common model is 30 in. wide and has four burners and a single oven. It's commonly a slide-in model with a raised backguard. Controls for oven and cooktop are located on the cooktop surface or on an apron. Knobs on aprons are easier to clean than knobs on cooktops; electronic keypads are even easier to clean. Drop-in ranges often have no backguard and offer the option of a cabinet drawer below the oven.

Wider ranges—from 36 in. to 60 in.—are tempting for their varied cooktop and oven options. Some manufacturers even offer dual-fuel ranges with a gas cooktop and electric oven—along with a considerably higher price tag.

▲ AN AGA RANGE LIKE THIS ONE IS ALWAYS READY TO GO, with multiple ovens capable of being set to various temperatures, from warm to hot. The flue circulates a constant flow of air through the cooker, venting odors and smoke outside.

◄ THESE SIMPLE INSET CABINETS ARE A SUBTLE FOIL for the punch of a professional-style range. Unlike its super-hot restaurant cousin, a professional-style range has insulated sides, which don't require clearance from cabinetry.

◀ A RANGE COULD HAVE FIT HERE, but instead separate cooktop and wall-oven units are stacked to make a streamlined alternative cooking space. Separate components also make a lighter burden to haul to a second-floor kitchen. The backsplash runs the full length and height of the wall for extra protection.

Commercial or Pro-Style?

COMMERCIAL RANGES—true professional models—may be tempting to the homeowner because of their blast-furnace power and relatively low price tags compared to professional-style home ranges. But today's professional-style ranges have lots of firepower and industrial good looks, along with safety features that you won't find on a commercial range.

The restaurant, or commercial, range is not insulated like a pro-style home range, so it can't be positioned near cabinets. Its pilot lights are always on (some do have electronic ignition), whereas pro-style ranges feature electronic igniters. Other drawbacks? Commercial ranges are deeper (almost 3 ft. deep if they have convection ovens), knobs are not child safe, and ovens have no windows, lights, or broilers.

You will see some commercial ranges in this book (all owned by people who have cooked in restaurants), but many municipalities don't allow—and insurance companies won't cover—commercial ranges in homes.

◀ A TRUE PROFESSIONAL RANGE IS A HOT BEAST, so it stands a requisite 3 in. from cabinetry, as seen here. Some cooks love the unbridled heat and are undaunted by hot surfaces, no oven windows, and always-on pilot lights.

▼ YOU MIGHT THINK THIS IS A PROFESSIONAL RANGE that found its way into a residential kitchen, but it's really a professional-style range, fitted with family-friendly features such as insulated sides and oven windows.

A BRICK BACKSPLASH AND A RANGE HOOD with lights top this Aga range. The hobs (burners) are covered to retain heat until ready to use, while the simmer plate at left has a range of heat available.

THIS VINTAGE GLENWOOD RANGE HAS FEATURES that few modern American ranges have, but that many European models offer. A lid covers the burners when not in use and an assemblage of oven sizes, particularly small ovens, offer energy efficiency.

THIS OLD RANGE HAS BEEN RESTORED to handle today's cooking needs, and it makes a great retro statement surrounded by white cabinets and subway tile.

Oven Options

OVENS ARE THE LEAST EFFICIENT COOKING APPLIANCES—standard large-cavity ovens may use only 10 to 28 percent of the energy expended—but they cost little to run. A smaller cavity improves efficiency and moisture retention. Several mid-to-high-end manufacturers offer ranges with a small oven paired with a large oven, typically side-by-side but occasionally stacked.

The conventional oven is a radiant, or thermal, oven, which cooks by a combination of radiant energy from a heat source and natural convection from heated air. If you broil frequently, look for adjustable broiler temperatures and an element with more loops, which allow for more even broiling.

▼THIS WIDE FIVE STAR RANGE HAS TWO BIG GAS OVENS and two broiling drawers. The lower counter to the left is sized to accommodate younger cooks learning the ropes.

Microwave Options

A MICROWAVE OVEN IS THE MOST COMMON SECOND OVEN in kitchens today. In addition to the basic models, there are several microwave-combination ovens that join microwave cooking with other types of heat. The variations include microwave/convection ovens, microwave/halogen ovens, and microwave/toaster ovens, which take microwaves beyond reheating and making popcorn into the realms of baking, browning, roasting, toasting, and even grilling. A medium-size (1.2 to 1.6 cu. ft.) combination oven can handle roasts and whole chickens.

Over-the-range (OTR) microwaves remain popular in small kitchens and can have a recirculating vent built into the bottom, but such vents are not strong enough for heavy-duty cooktop wizardry. OTR microwaves are also too high for some cooks and may pose traffic conflicts in two-cook kitchens.

Built-in microwave ovens look attractive, but most models are deeper than 15-in. wall cabinets; that's why more micro-wave ovens are making an appearance in base cabinets or island cabinetry. The right-hinged microwave door remains as elusive as Bigfoot, but several microwave and microwave-combination ovens hinge on the bottom (not OTR models), which can be handy for undercounter or countertop use.

WHEN THE MICROWAVE IS NEEDED, a flip-up door slides completely out of the way into the cabinet. At other times the microwave is hidden behind the flipper door.

RATHER THAN TAKE UP COUNTERTOP SPACE in a small kitchen, a microwave oven fits into a cabinet with a trim kit that allows for ventilation. The compactly designed corner is packed with a pantry at left, cookbook shelves and a phone cubby, a bulletin board, several drawers, and a niche behind the microwave for the cat to dine.

Ovens: Gas or Electric?

CHOOSING A FUEL SOURCE FOR AN OVEN doesn't seem to rile up cooks as much as the cooktop heat source, but there's still a decided tilt toward electric ovens. Electric ovens produce a more even heat (particularly convection ovens, which are electric). Gas ovens have a moister heat, which can be a bonus, and they have a slight edge in terms of installation cost; an electric oven requires a 220-volt circuit while a gas oven uses a standard 110-volt circuit.

If location matters, keep in mind that wall ovens are electric while range ovens can be either gas or electric. Whichever you choose, don't base your choice on a model that says it will preheat in just minutes—nearly all ovens need an additional 10 to 20 minutes after they signal readiness to be truly heated through and through.

▶ NOSTALGIC FOR HER EXPERIENCE cooking in an Italian brick oven, a Rhode Island cook had this wood-fired brick oven installed in a contemporary kitchen. The flue on the outside of the oven effectively exhausts the smoke from the wood fire so that heat isn't lost from the oven itself. The owners bake everything in this oven, including cakes, casseroles, roasts, and, of course, pizza.

▼ THIS MICROWAVE FITS INTO A GENERIC-SIZE COMPARTMENT, allowing for easy replacement if necessary. The leftover space makes a first-rate spot to store a cutting board for use on the slate countertop. The wall opens to the primary dishwashing sink. An Aga range is the centerpiece of the cooking part of the kitchen.

The Warming Oven

A WARMING OVEN **can be a much-appreciated addition to a family kitchen, where activity and mealtime schedules tend to get complicated. Even though some standard-size ovens can be set to the low temperatures of a warming oven, the smaller chamber of the latter keeps food moist longer, and most models have an adjustable humidity control.**

Check the temperature range of models as you shop; bakers, for instance, may wish for a temperature below 100°F for proofing bread.

Location should be based on use. A warming oven directly below or across from the cooktop or oven makes things easy for the cook, but putting it between the kitchen and dining area gives family members easier access.

▲ A WARMING DRAWER FITS EASILY INTO THIS ISLAND, which is situated in a triangle with both cooktop and wall ovens, and it's easy to access from the dining area.

Cooktop Options

NOT ONLY ARE MOST MEALS MADE ON A COOKTOP, but it's also a high-visibility item, so it makes sense to choose one with the right balance of looks, performance, and ease of cleaning. The first decision used to be between gas or electric, but while most cooktops are still either all gas or all electric, there are now dual-fuel cooktops that combine gas burners with electric elements below ceramic glass.

Another thing to consider is control location. Apron controls are easier to clean and won't get in the way of cooking, but they're more accessible to kids (many models have lock-out features). Cooktop controls can be easier to access, but they take up valuable cooktop space. Controls on the backguard are relatively childproof, but they can get mighty dirty and can be blocked by big pots. The choice of knobs or electronic control pads depends on looks and what you're comfortable operating.

▲ THIS SMOOTHTOP COOKTOP WITH A DOWNDRAFT VENT is so subtle that you'd hardly notice its presence, except for the gently arched cabinet above, where a light is hidden.

◄ A CERAMIC-GLASS SMOOTHTOP IS SET IN TILE in a family kitchen. A raised wall behind will help the downdraft vent work more efficiently and shield cooking from other activities.

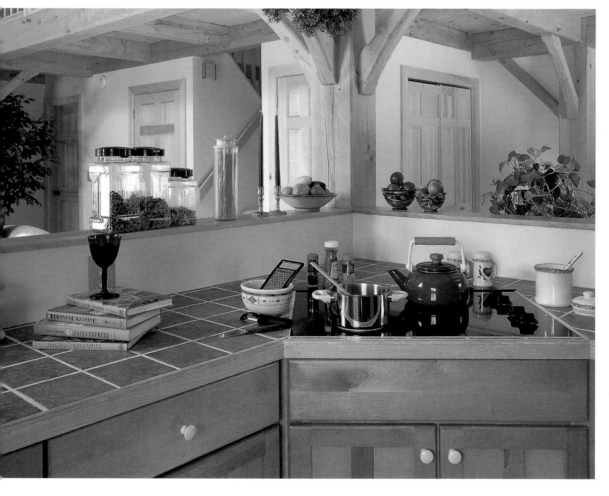

Gas Cooktops

IN ADDITION TO BEING CHEAPER to operate in many parts of the country, the biggest advantage of gas cooktops is that they provide immediate, easily adjustable heat that can be instantly turned off. They can take on many shapes and styles, and grates can cover the whole cooktop or just the burner. The continuous grate allows pots to sit anywhere, but also makes more surfaces to clean. Matte black grates are much easier to keep looking clean than light-colored grates.

Today's gas burners can be sealed, which many people prefer because spills stay on the surface instead of pooling into a netherworld below, and heat is more efficiently directed to the pan (an unsealed burner can lose as much as 1/4 of its heat). Some manufacturers offer a combination of burners on the same cooktop, from as low as 400 Btu (British thermal units) to 18,000 Btu (15,000 Btu is the max for most pro-style cooktops). Both these extremes tend to be found on pricier professional-style cooktops; standard gas cooktop burners run from 9,000 to 12,000 Btu maximum. Some cooks prefer the flexibility of all burners having the same power.

Many cooks supplement burners with cooktop accessories such as grills and griddles. A grill can be adapted for griddle cooking simply by using a cast-iron griddle on top. Simmer plates (also called French plates) cover a high-Btu burner (plates are removable for direct cooking) to provide various levels of heat for pots and pans—high in the center and simmering at the edges. Wok rings allow for steady wok cooking over the hottest gas burners. Cooktop rotisseries are available for a few high-end models.

◄ A DROP-IN GAS COOKTOP HAS JUST A MODICUM of the industrial look but all the speed and adjustability of a pro-style gas range. This drop-in cooktop doesn't have a pop-up downdraft vent, but a range hood is more efficient anyway—and it's a thing of beauty with a copper patina.

◄ A LARGE COOKTOP CAN TAKE UP A BIG CHUNK OF THE ISLAND, but it provides maximum capacity for people who take their cooking seriously. It has a grill and four burners and two downdraft vents (black, rather than white, was a good choice here).

◄ THIS DOWNDRAFT GAS COOKTOP IS SET in a soapstone-topped island. The design of this kitchen is in keeping with the rest of the house, inspired by the English architect C.F.A. Voysey, who was known for designing Arts and Crafts-style manors.

► A RANGE WITH A VIEW MAKES IT TOUGHER for a range hood to do an efficient job, but an 8-in. jump in countertop heights helps funnel steam and grease upward. This detail also shields counter sitters from the cooktop. The range hood is slim and elegant enough not to be a visual obstruction, and it is wide enough to provide effective ventilation. Hood lights are essential here, since no other task lighting is available.

▶ A HIGH-POWERED WOK BURNER IS A DREAM OF MANY, and here the dream has come true. Both the range and the wok cooker are professional appliances—not professional-style—so they require extra attention and forethought in the planning stages. A serious ventilation system hides behind the wood valence.

Electric Cooktops

POPULAR SMOOTHTOPS have ceramic-glass surfaces that cover radiant-heat electric coils, disks, or ribbons. High-priced, super-fast smoothtops may feature halogen lights or induction elements. Some love the way smoothtops clean and some dislike how easily they show smudges. Electric burners have been beefed up to suit high-heat cooking; the maximum is about 2,400w, which equals a 15,000-Btu gas burner. For safety, an electric cooktop should have indicator lights that show which burners are on or still hot. Look for a bridge element or elongated burners that allow for big containers, such as a roasting pan, and use cast iron pans on these tops with caution, as they can scratch the surface.

Induction cooktops are better known in Europe and restaurant kitchens. An induction cooktop has a smooth ceramic-glass top and uses electricity to generate a magnetic field that reacts with a ferrous pot or pan, which in turn heats the food. When the pan is taken off the burner, only residual heat from the pan remains, so you won't burn your hand on the cooktop. Chefs use induction cooktops frequently for the quick reaction time (rivaling gas), super-high heat, and low simmer. One drawback to an induction cooktop (aside from a high price tag) has been that only

flat-bottomed, ferrous cookware heats properly. That complaint has been addressed with the introduction of the wok-friendly induction cooktop, which features a concave burner that heats the whole wok in true stir-fry fashion.

▲ A SMOOTHTOP ELECTRIC COOKTOP IS AN IDEAL look for a contemporary kitchen. Locating it in a peninsula makes it tougher to ventilate, but that job is beautifully handled by a sleek-looking stainless-steel cylinder with glass surround.

◀ TWO SEPARATE TWO-BURNER COOKTOPS on a maple countertop provide plenty of cooking power for a small family, supplemented by a microwave below the counter and wall ovens (not seen) that share the same landing space as the microwave.

▲ A VIEW OF NARRAGANSETT BAY IS TOO GOOD to miss for an enthusiastic cook, so this professional-style cooktop is situated on a large island with a curved, raised countertop behind it. The raised countertop makes a subtle barrier between cooking and observing. Cabinets below the cooktop apron contain deep drawers for pots and pans.

Ventilation

CHOOSING THE PROPER SIZE VENT depends on the size and location of the cooktop, the type of vent, what kind of cooking you do, and the configuration of the exhaust pipe. A cooktop in an alcove allows for much more efficient venting than a cooktop in an island, which is subject to cross drafts. The closer a hood is to the cooktop, the better it works, but that may not suit tall cooks. Some cooktops are fitted with downdraft ventilation systems integrated into the cooktop, or with a pop-up or fixed vent along the back. Many homeowners like downdraft vents for islands because they think a big hood will block the view, but an island makes it tougher for downdraft vents to work well. It may be necessary to beef up the fan of an island downdraft vent.

▲ THESE RANGE-HOOD LIGHTS SHINE NOT ONLY on the cooktop but on brilliant Spanish tiles. The racks are bolted through the tile into 2x6 blocks that were retrofitted between studs.

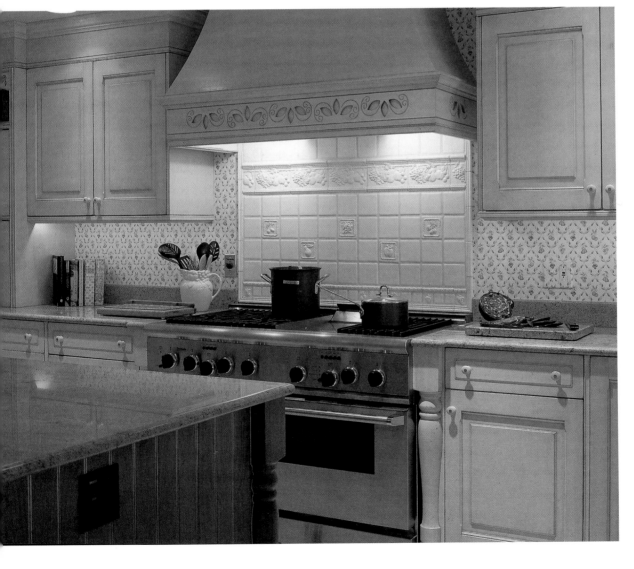

◄ A RANGE HOOD CAN TAKE ON THE RAIMENT of its surroundings. This hood is fitted with trim to match the cabinetry.

VENTING COOKTOPS

AN ISLAND COOKTOP NEEDS MORE VENTILATION.
Island ventilation systems have to fight cross currents,
so beef up the fan or make the hood opening wider and lower.

CHIMNEY-STYLE RANGE HOODS
The most effective way to vent cooktops.

Hoods can be installed from 18 in. to 36 in. above the cooktop,
depending on fan power. It's easy to remember: low power,
lower hood; high power, higher hood.

The wider the hood,
the higher it can
be positioned.

Extend the hood 3 in. past the cooktop for
more effective ventilation. A wider hood
can be installed higher above the cooktop.

**SURFACE-MOUNTED
DOWNDRAFT VENTS**
Can be located in the center
or back of the cooktop. These are
slightly less effective than pop-up
downdraft vents.

POP-UP DOWNDRAFT VENTS
Work well for lower pans and
low-fat cooking. These are often
chosen when a range hood is deemed
unsightly, but they aren't as effective.

▲ MUCH BIGGER THAN THE COOK-TOP IT COVERS, this copper hood is more than mere ventilation. It also provides task lighting for the whole island and ambient lighting for the whole kitchen.

▲ THIS FURNITURE-LIKE HOOD COVER HIDES a high-powered ventilation system so that it's easy to cook on a pro-style cooktop while maintaining the look of a genteel, traditional kitchen.

◄ GLASS EXTENDS THE REACH OF THIS VENT HOOD without adding bulk and makes a sparkling surface for lighting. A full tile backsplash with a row of handmade copper and silver accent tiles picks up metallic flecks in the granite countertop. The tile continues past the edge of the hood to provide full protection from steam and grease.

A MILE-LONG HOOD VENTS A MULTITUDE of cooking appliances, including two cooktops and two ovens. Two wall ovens add even more cooking power to this log house.

LOCATING THE RANGE AGAINST THE BACK OF A FIREPLACE allows the range hood to piggyback on the chimney space, and the wall makes for much more efficient venting, along with shielding cooking from the dining room.

Refrigerators

THE STANDARD REFRIGERATOR has the freezer on top, which is the least expensive and most common model. However, a bottom-freezer refrigerator is easier on your back; look for a model with a pull-out drawer, as fixed shelves are tough to access. Side-by-side models are the least efficient as far as energy and space go, but are popular (see the sidebar on the facing page). Having a separate full-height freezer and fridge might be the best choice for active cooking and entertaining. Besides offering plenty of space, this admittedly expensive arrangement ensures that there's no crossbreeding of temperatures or smells.

Fridges can be built in or freestanding. Freestanding models are less expensive and bulkier—they'll stand out from the cabinetry. Built-in refrigerators—these are usually side-by-side or bottom freezer—are taller than freestanding models but not as deep, so they can be designed flush with cabinetry and fitted with matching panels.

▼ DESPITE ITS RETRO CHARM, IF YOU OPENED up this fridge you'd see humidity-control crispers, slide-out glass shelves, and bins with gallon-size storage—all the bells and whistles found in the most modern refrigerators. Both the Heartland refrigerator and its mate, a range with electric solid-disk cooktop, have an enamel finish with nickel-plated trim.

A BUILT-IN REFRIGERATOR CAN BE FITTED WITH ANY KIND of panel to take on any look you like. This fridge is finished in the whimsical style throughout the kitchen.

Pros and Cons of Side-by-Sides

SIDE-BY-SIDE REFRIGERATORS fill many needs, but may not be for everyone. Side-by-side aficionados will argue that their model is easier on the back because you can organize both fridge and freezer with most-used items around eye level. Other virtues are that side-by-side doors are narrower and therefore don't swing out far, narrow shelves are easier to pull out to access and wash (if pull-out shelves are available), they more easily accommodate in-door ice and water dispensers and optional water filters (these can take up as much as a quarter of available freezer space, however), and they're more accessible to people with physical disabilities (it might give parents pause to know that little kids find them easier to open, too).

Still, in addition to costing more to buy and run, many side-by-side models aren't wide enough on either side for party platters or big frozen pizzas, and if your heart is set on a counter-depth model, a standard 36-in. side-by-side may not have enough room overall. To solve the riddle of which model to buy, measure the space you have available for the fridge and for door swings, and try out favorite pans and party platters in refrigerators at an appliance store.

A SIDE-BY-SIDE FRIDGE MAKES SENSE in a smaller kitchen like this one. Open doors take up less aisle room. This built-in model is 24 in. deep and 3 ft. wide.

Look at the Yellow Tag

THAT YELLOW TAG on each refrigerator in an appliance showroom is the EnergyGuide, which allows consumers to compare energy costs. Numbers on the tag include the energy use of the model in kilowatt-hours per year (kWh/year). A refrigerator rated for 425 kWh/year has an estimated power use of ten 100-watt light bulbs left on for 425 hours. Another number on the tag estimates annual cost in dollars, but the federal average for energy use may not relate to what you pay in your municipality, which can be as much as three times the U.S. average rate.

Depending on the age of your current refrigerator, buying a new model can actually be a money-saving enterprise over a few years. New refrigerators have a federally imposed mandate to be much more efficient than their ancestors, even those made just a year ago. See the Sources section on p. 186 for the government's Energy Star program.

▲ A SIDE-BY-SIDE REFRIGERATOR ALLOWS DINERS easy access to cold water and ice on the outside and food on the inside. The brilliance of the stainless steel provides a cool color contrast to the warm tones of cabinetry, wall, and floor.

► IT'S HARD TO IMAGINE THAT THIS REFRIGERATOR once had black panels. Now it is paneled with reclaimed, refinished barn lumber, mostly pine. Handles are branches that are sanded and polyurethaned.

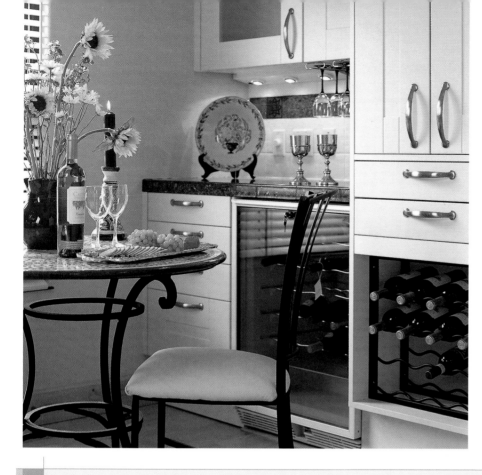

◄ A CORNER OF THE KITCHEN/ DINING AREA DESIGNATED for the appreciation of wine is fitted with a wine cooler. These units can be controlled to maintain the perfect temperature for whatever type of wine you chose. A lock is a handy feature.

Refrigerator Drawers

THE REFRIGERATOR DRAWER is a brilliant revolution in cooling technology. A refrigerator or freezer drawer can be placed just about anywhere convenience dictates. In a smaller kitchen, freezer drawers can be paired with an undercounter refrigerator to keep walls free of cabinetry or appliances.

► THIS NEW HOUSE IN NANTUCKET HAS THE CHARACTER of a summer cottage but all the conveniences are under the counter, hidden behind cabinet doors. An undercounter refrigerator and two refrigerator drawers are built into the island.

A FULL-SIZE REFRIGERATOR AND A SEPARATE FREEZER are built into a 10-ft.-tall cabinet with frosted-glass doors and birch veneer case and doors. The assembly is scaled to fit a large kitchen built for big parties.

THIS HIGH-EFFICIENCY REFRIGERATOR (SUNFROST) IS FINISHED with a copper veneer that has been given a patina with heat and chemicals. Handles are turned walnut. Countertops are solid surface and stainless steel.

WHAT COULD BE MORE IDEAL THAN AN ALL-FREEZER unit and an all-refrigerator unit side-by-side? These have a landing space opposite and to the right. Compressors are on the bottom, so there's room for cabinetry above.

◄ BUILT-IN REFRIGERATORS LIKE THIS ONE HAVE COM-PRESSORS at the top to reduce the depth of the appliance. That makes for a fairly toasty atmosphere, so this wine-storage cabinet is for everyday wines.

▼ THIS BIG COMMERCIAL REFRIGERATOR ADDS A PLEAS-ING contrast in this refined log house. The refrigerator half has a glass door for easy viewing, while the freezer has a solid stainless door.

Floors, Walls, and Ceilings

Surrounding all the handsome cabinetry, generous countertops, and sparkling appliances is the skin of the kitchen: floor, walls, and ceiling. Glossy or matte, smooth or rough textured, these surfaces will have a significant role in shaping the style and ambience of the kitchen, not to mention ease—or difficulty—of maintenance. Floors, especially, require as much deliberation as choosing a cooktop or a countertop.

Consider floor, wall, and ceiling finishes early in the design process. Flooring is a key player in coordinating construction schedules, and it's also important to know if any special finishes, such as veneer plaster, wainscoting, or beadboard paneling, will be applied before plumbing, HVAC, and electrical are roughed out in walls and ceilings.

Final finishes, such as paint, wallpaper, and trim, can wait until later in the building process, which is a blessing. As a real-life kitchen takes shape, it often looks different from its representation on paper and in 3-D computer modeling, and the quality of light and space might suggest some adjustments to finishes.

◀ A VARIETY OF COLORS AND TEXTURES ON FLOORS, walls, and ceilings brighten an almost all-wood kitchen. In keeping with the Craftsman-style details, the floor is strip oak, stained to be medium dark. The ceiling acquires a pizzazz of its own with elaborate molding on the beams and painted beadboard in the recesses. Around the cooking alcove, the wall is finished with skim-coat plaster that's given a painted, weathered appearance that recalls the days of cooking in a fireplace.

Choosing a Floor

CHOOSING A FLOOR DEPENDS ON YOUR COMFORT LEVEL, not only with standing but with maintenance, as a kitchen floor takes a thrashing. Also consider looks, cost, and installation techniques. Resilient floors offer easy installation and economy, while solid wood continues to have cachet—especially reclaimed wide-board floors. Laminate flooring and floating floors are new kids on the block with a growing following, while tile and stone are old favorites, renowned for being not only beautiful, but tough against water, stains, and wear and tear. Concrete is both a new favorite and an old one, as mid-20th-century Modernism is seeing a renaissance.

Many flooring types can be installed over existing floors if the floor is intact and smooth, but it's worth consulting an expert first. If a new floor is going in over an old floor, have flooring or a same-height subfloor installed under moveable appliances to ease repair or replacement.

▼ RECTANGULAR FIELD TILES— USED IN THE BACKGROUND— are light-colored slate, while dark slate squares make a border around the island. Dark and light tiles fill in with a diagonal checkerboard. Slate, like most stone, must be sealed to prevent staining.

▲ TILE AND WOOD ABUT IN A HANDSOME, PRACTICAL way in a big family kitchen and eating area. Tile bordered by stone covers the workspace, while wood finishes off the eating and family areas.

▶ A BLUE ANILINE DYE FOLLOWED BY SATIN POLYURETHANE finishes a strip-maple floor to make a surface that shimmers. It makes a cool contrast to cream-colored cabinetry and solid-surface countertops. By the way, refrigerator drawers in the foreground are disguised with wood panels.

Which Comes First, Cabinets or Floor?

YOU WON'T FIND A CONSENSUS ON the issue of whether to install cabinets or flooring first. If cabinets go in first, the floor won't get damaged by dropped tools or equipment, and expensive flooring materials are not hidden under cabinets. But installing the floor first makes the job easier, and labor will cost less because flooring materials won't need to be fitted around the base cabinets. Flooring can help protect the structure against leaking appliances, too, and the appliances won't be hemmed in by flooring, nor will there be awkward flooring changes if cabinets are removed during remodeling.

In the case of an especially expensive flooring material, an alternative is to mark the cabinet footprints and fill those portions with plywood to the thickness of the finished floor, being sure to account for recessed toe kicks on cabinets and appliances. Make sure the installed floor is well protected during the rest of construction, however.

▲THIS KITCHEN FEATURES TWO MATERIALS designed to look like slate but are much less expensive. Ceramic tile on backsplash and countertops mimics slate and the textured vinyl-tile flooring looks uncannily like slate laid with no grout lines.

Vinyl, Linoleum, and Cork Flooring

CLASSIFIED AS A FLEXIBLE, thin material that is glued to the subfloor, resilient flooring includes vinyl tile, sheet vinyl, linoleum, cork, and rubber. Many of these flexible materials are also available glued to a plank or tile-sized panel and installed as floating floors (see the sidebar on p. 155).

Vinyl is the easiest to install and is hence the most common kitchen flooring. It's also relatively soft underfoot. Because it has few or no joints (some rolls are as wide as 12 ft.), sheet vinyl is more water resistant than vinyl tile. The cheapest vinyl is flimsy, tends to yellow, and is easy to scratch, but high-priced vinyl flooring is very durable, colorfast, and handsome—and still a lot less expensive than most flooring materials. Inlaid colors and patterns have a much thicker layer of color than surface-printed styles. Avoid rubber- or latex-backed mats or area rugs as the backing can stain a vinyl floor.

Linoleum is made from linseed oil and pulverized, naturally occurring materials, including cork, wood, and limestone. Linoleum was upstaged by vinyl for years, but it has come into its own again with a no-wax surface and many rich colors. Available in sheets up to 7 ft. wide and in 13-in. tiles, linoleum has through-the-body color and it is durable, quiet, hypoallergenic, and easy on the standing cook's feet and legs. Its price tag is higher than vinyl, however, and it requires an expert to install in glue-down form.

Cork has seen a century of service as a warm-looking, quiet, reasonably durable, and comfortable floor—and it still does, but with enhanced performance. Today's cork flooring is sealed with urethane so that it is moisture-resistant and doesn't require the regular waxing that older cork floors did. Cork is traditionally installed as solid tiles that are glued down; now it is also available as floating-floor planks, with a layer of cork laminated to a substrate.

◄LINOLEUM TILES LAID IN A CHECKBOARD PATTERN make a warm-looking, hypoallergenic, and comfortable floor. Today's easy-care linoleum is finished in the factory and doesn't need the frequent waxing that sent linoleum into retirement in the mid-1900s.

Laminate Flooring

LAMINATE FLOORING is made up of a clear wear layer, a photographed paper layer, a product-panel core, and a backing, preferably a water-resistant plastic. The photographed layer can look like anything, but wood, stone, and tile are by far the most common. Flooring is available as planks (these look like wood), square tiles (stone), and occasionally larger rectangular blocks that look like stone or wood.

Laminate floors are relatively comfortable to stand on and can be very durable and water resistant, depending on the quality of the laminate sandwich and the installation method. In most cases laminate flooring is installed as a floating floor (see the sidebar on the facing page).

◀ IN THIS URBAN KITCHEN, LARGE VINYL TILES make a stonelike floor in accord with stone drawer and door knobs and stone countertops.

What Is a Floating Floor?

FLOATING FLOORS CAN BE SOLID WOOD, engineered wood, cork, vinyl, linoleum, bamboo, or rubber, but not brittle materials. A floating floor doesn't really hover, it just isn't attached to the substrate. Floating-floor manufacturers say their floors can be installed over a plywood substrate or a concrete slab (vapor barrier required), or just about any old flooring material that's reasonably smooth, flat, and dry. Individual planks or tiles in a floating floor are linked together by glue or by various mechanical connections—look for words like "click" and "lock." Glue may be a better choice in a kitchen that will see lots of cooking. The perimeter of a floating floor must be shy of the wall by a few millimeters to allow for expansion. Floating floors can almost float if installed on a thin layer of resilient foam.

Individual pieces are tiles, boards, or large panels.

Top layer is any fairly flexible material: wood, cork, vinyl, linoleum, bamboo, or rubber.

A floating floor isn't attached to the substrate, so it is easy to install and easy to replace.

Pieces are joined by a mechanical connection such as tongue-and-groove. Joints are glued for a more water-resistant floor.

Base is a panel product such as medium-density fiberboard.

Install over plywood, concrete slab, or preexisting flooring that is smooth and flat. Install over a layer of resilient foam for more cushioning.

WOOD FLOORS

◄ A WIDE-PLANK PINE FLOOR COM-PLETES the all-wood effect in this breakfast room filled with pine wainscoting and oak furniture.

▲ THIS OLD PINE FLOOR GETS A FACE-LIFT with a checkerboard pattern painted with translucent white and blue glaze. Polyure-thane protects the paint layer.

▶ RUNNING THIS WIDE-PLANK PINE FLOOR from the family/dining area through the kitchen makes the space appear more generous. More formal pine-strip flooring takes over at the edge of the kitchen and covers the living room floor.

More on Wood Floors

WOOD HAS SEEN A REVIVAL as kitchen floor material in North America, appreciated for its traditional beauty, resilience underfoot, and ability to be refinished. The downside of wood is that it is relatively soft and can be scratched, especially when big dogs and sand are prevalent. But wood floors can look great in an active kitchen if properly finished.

Strip flooring—¾-in.-thick and 2½-in.-wide—is the most common wood flooring, while plank flooring—from 3 in. to 10 in.—is more expensive but much admired. Be aware that in low humidity, wide-plank floors will develop wider gaps than strip flooring. Most wood floors are hardwood, with red and white oak the standard species for strip flooring. Oak is dimensionally stable relative to other species, and it is receptive to sanding, staining, and finishing. Plank flooring is available in oak, maple, cherry, and hickory, while hardier softwoods, such as heart pine and fir, make beautiful traditional plank floors.

Proper installation and finishing make all the difference in a long-lasting wood floor. Before it is installed, wood flooring must become acclimated to the house (acclimation time depends on climate, wood species, and the age of the wood). Oil-based urethane makes a softer, deeper-looking finish that's easy to touch up but takes longer to dry, while water-based urethane has a milder odor, dries quickly (this can also make it tricky to apply), and makes a harder skin on the surface. Moisture-cured urethane makes the toughest and most moisture-resistant finish, but it is expensive and difficult to apply, not to mention toxic smelling during curing. Grit and water can damage any wood floor finish, so frequent vacuuming and prompt attention to spills are important. Area rugs can help out in front of the sources of water and grime, such as sinks and cooktops.

STRIP FLOORING

2½-in.-wide and ¾-in.-thick strip flooring with tongue-and-groove edges nailed to subfloor.

All wood floors expand and contract with humidity changes. Floors should be laid shy of walls to allow for this expansion. Cover joints with baseboard.

PLANK (BOARD) FLOORING

Planks are 3 in. to 7 in. or wider and ½-in. to 1-in. thick with tongue-and-groove edges nailed to subfloor. Planks can be random width or same width.

To keep especially wide boards from cupping, ends can be screwed to subflooring and capped with wood plugs.

ENGINEERED WOOD FLOORING

Engineered wood is more stable than solid wood but can't be refinished as many times.

Strips, panels, or parquet tiles can be installed as glue-down systems or floating-floor systems.

Thin layer of wood is laminated to plywood backing.

Engineered Wood

Engineered-wood flooring is really a version of plywood with a top layer of wood laminate that's thick enough to refinish two or three times. Individual pieces can look like single strips or planks or can look like several strips glued together. Products are available prefinished or unfinished and as glue-down systems or floating-floor systems. Engineered-wood floors are more dimensionally stable than wood and are permitted below grade, where conditions may be damp, so they can be a good choice in the kitchen.

▲ THIS WIDE-BOARD SOFTWOOD FLOOR IN A 200-YEAR-OLD house received a soft blue-green paint that brightens the floor with a minimum of labor.

▲ A DARK STAIN TAKES THIS OAK-STRIP FLOOR from ordinary to interesting and provides a chromatic balance between the light cabinets and black countertops.

◄ STRIP-WOOD FLOORING STOPS AT THE THRESHOLD of this contemporary kitchen. From there, the floor is built up of end-grain wood blocks laminated together. End-grain wood is hard as nails and should last a long, long time.

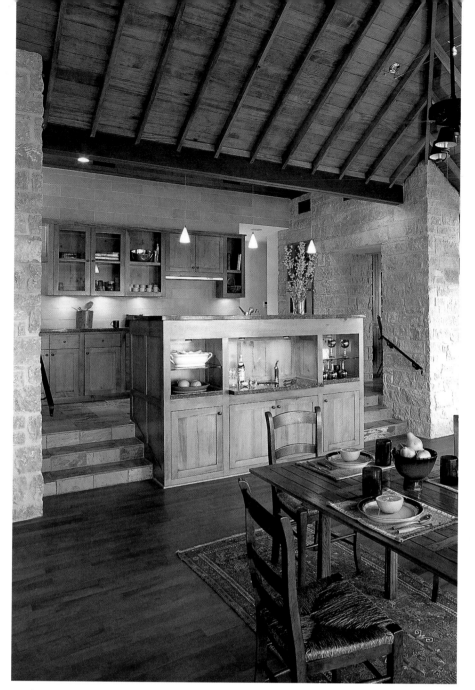

◀ IN A TEXAS HILL-COUNTRY HOUSE, MESQUITE is a natural for flooring. This dining room floor is richly figured and durable. Kitchen flooring is slate tile and walls are limestone.

▼ STRIP-WOOD FLOORING IS A WARM, RELATIVELY easy to clean, comfortable flooring for a kitchen. It's especially appropriate in a traditionally styled kitchen.

Bamboo Floors

IT MAY TECHNICALLY BE A GRASS rather than a tree, but bamboo has only a bit more cellulose than wood and shares many characteristics. Bamboo is touted as an environmentally friendly flooring, as "timber" bamboo is plantation grown and grows like wildfire (it's not the species that pandas eat).

Because it is narrow, bamboo is laminated vertically and horizontally. Vertical-grain bamboo has a linear look—think edge-grain butcher block—while horizontal-grain bamboo shows the distinctive bamboo knuckles. Edges can be square (unfinished) or microbeveled (finished), and unfinished bamboo can be stained (with certain dye-based stains) and finished like wood. Glue-down, nail-down, and floating-floor systems are available.

TILE & STONE FLOORS

▶ THE TILE FLOOR IN THIS RENO-VATED KITCHEN reflects light from new skylights. These 12-in.-square ceramic tiles are textured for ease of walking and standing, and grout lines are tinted a gray-green, which hides dirt better while complementing the greens in surrounding elements.

More on Tile and Stone

TILE AND STONE FLOORS ARE BEAUTIFUL, durable, and long-lived, but hard on both dropped dishes and your legs and back, although they can be softened up a bit with area rugs. Tile's toughness and thermal qualities make it a favorite in beach-house kitchens and in the warm climates of the Southwest and West. Any kind of tile or stone retains heat, so it is ideal for radiant-heat floors. Stone is as strong as tile, but it isn't always as resistant to stains and water, so most stones must be sealed periodically. Tile that looks like stone is a hardy and more economical alternative.

Not all tile is the same. Ceramic tile has a glazed layer over a white clay body, while porcelain tile and quarry tiles have color through the body so chips won't be as apparent. Grout lines are the weak link in stone and tile floors and should always be sealed to reduce the tendency to stain. Choose a tinted grout over white grout for additional defense against wear and tear. Larger tiles, whether stone or ceramic, look elegant and have the added benefit of fewer grout lines. One popular trend is to lay tiles close together with thin or no grout lines.

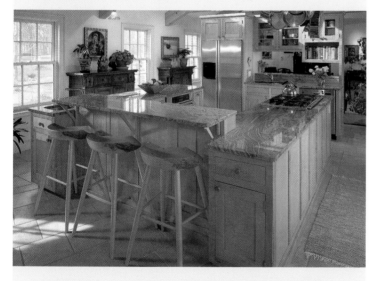

▲ GLAZED CERAMIC TILE CAN LOOK LIKE STONE, but it's actually easier to care for, as it needs no sealant and is less expensive. This subdued tile makes a backdrop for a dramatically grained stone countertop.

▲ THIS BOLD TILE PATTERN FITS PERFECTLY in a large kitchen with soaring ceilings, a huge arched window, and a statuesque china hutch.

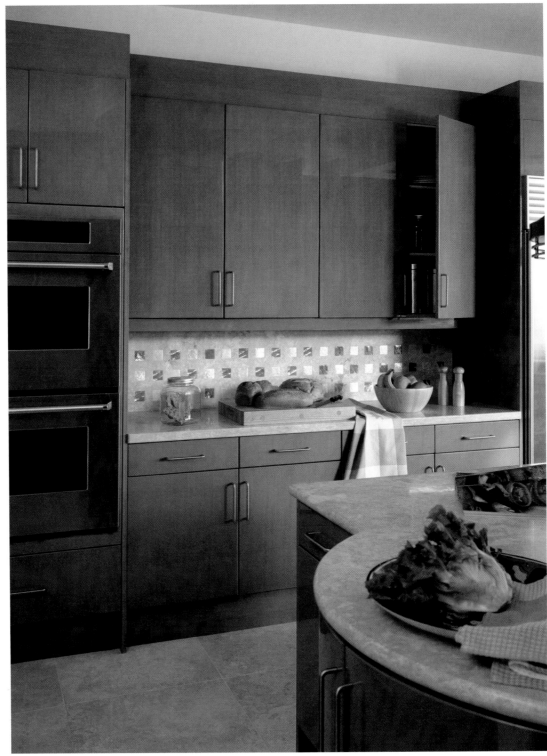

THIS DURANGO LIMESTONE IS FAIRLY POROUS, but a sealer applied periodically makes it easy to care for. Countertops and backsplashes are made from the same limestone, although the backsplash is inset with squares of dark and light mother-of-pearl squares.

TILE LENDS ITSELF TO A BORDER DESIGN, but here a wood border is used around cabinets. The foot or so of wood makes a more comfortable place to stand and work and also gives the tile a more prominent role.

CONCRETE FLOORING

◀ THIS CONCRETE FLOOR IN A BUSY FAMILY KITCHEN is finished minimally, with two coats of boiled linseed oil, a finish that isn't as stainproof as sealer, but that makes a softer sheen. The slab is imbedded with radiant-heat polyethylene tubing. Color was added to the concrete after pouring, allowing for the use of two colors. The border pattern ties together the kitchen cabinets and gives an impression similar to a large oriental rug.

▶ A GRID OF WOOD STRIPS IS CAST INTO THE blue-tinted concrete floor to effectively make small concrete slabs. Providing such control joints minimizes or even prevents cracking.

More on Concrete

CONCRETE IS CAPTIVATING because of its chameleon-like quality in taking on color and texture and its compatibility with both traditional and modern kitchens. It's a durable surface, particularly when sealed, and it's ideal for radiant-heat flooring because tubing can be integral with the floor. Keep in mind that placing a concrete floor calls for a pause in kitchen construction, so plan accordingly. Concrete takes several days to prep, place, and cut control joints, and then it must not be covered for at least ten days. When it is covered, avoid debris and overlapping joints that can telegraph onto the curing slab.

Concrete can look luxurious with color added. Pigments added to the mix will be uniform, while color that is troweled on after placing or acid etched after curing can be uniform or intentionally mottled in the manner of marble or a watercolor painting.

A concrete floor will thrive with proper preparation and maintenance. Membrane sealers protect against acids and oils, which are tough on concrete, but are shiny and can scratch easily (some concrete aficionados liken these to plastic slipcovers on a couch). Penetrating sealers are less resistant to acids and oils, but they don't scratch like membrane sealers and they allow color and texture to show. Whatever the sealer, it must be reapplied periodically.

Concrete will crack, so plan for control joints.

Rule of thumb for locating joints: multiply concrete thickness in inches times 32 and divide by 12. A 2-in. slab will need a 5-ft. grid of control joints.

Concrete is ideal for radiant-heat tubing.

Color can be integral with concrete mix or can be applied during or after curing. Seal concrete to minimize staining.

Joints should be sawn soon after concrete is placed, or joints can be formed by casting metal or wood strips in a grid or decorative pattern. In a kitchen, sawn control joints are often grouted to prevent debris from falling in.

Walls and Ceilings

CONSIDERING THE IMPACT WALLS AND CEILINGS HAVE on the ambience of a kitchen, give them attention early in the design process. Faux painting and stenciling add color and interest, while wallpaper, wainscoting, and other surface-applied treatments not only add style, but can provide a durable surface. Take into account the orientation of your kitchen when choosing colors. A north-facing kitchen benefits from light, warm colors, while a south-facing kitchen may call for a cooler hue. If paint or wallpaper is the choice for a backsplash, go for satin or glossy paint or water-resistant wallpaper for ease of cleaning.

A ceiling offers opportunity for structural—or faux structural—embellishment. Exposed beams provide a place to hang pots and light fixtures and add warmth and coziness to a tall space. A coved ceiling makes a room more formal and spacious, and it can be embellished with a painted frieze and concealed lighting.

▲ A WOOD-PANELED FRIEZE AT THE TOP OF THE WALL cabinets adds an unexpected touch with stenciled gold lines from Frost's poem, *The Road Not Taken*, perhaps to encourage the family to cook outside the box.

◄ AT JUST OVER 9 FT. HIGH, THIS RICH RED CEILING enlivens a large, curved kitchen, adding depth and preventing the space from feeling too big. Countertops are soapstone and strip-wood flooring is Douglas fir.

◀ PAINT TAKES THIS KITCHEN INTO WHIMSICAL REALMS, along with the fancifully cut wood applied to cabinets and walls.

▲ THE GLOSSY, WHITE BEADBOARD CEILING in this airy kitchen reflects light from corner windows and cove lights, making a bright balance to the wood tones of floor and cabinets.

▶ THE DRAMA AND BEAUTY OF A TREE-TRUNK POST called for something more than the standard drywall ceiling. A gently arched strip-oak ceiling calls up the image of curves on a boat. Coved edges provide space for lighting and beveled skylights are custom designed to fit the ceiling.

▼A BASEMENT DOOR THAT DOESN'T GET MUCH USE doubles as wall space when it is glazed with panes of commercial-grade chalkboard to make a family message center in a busy kitchen.

▲WHITE OAK FLOORS WITH A GLOSSY FINISH and glossy white paint on ceilings reflect light beautifully in this renovated Craftsman-style kitchen. New shallow box beams (mahogany to match the cabinets) are fitted with custom-designed Arts and Crafts–style ceiling fixtures.

▶THESE EMBOSSED METAL CEILING TILES with metal cove trim make a dazzling and heat-resistant kitchen ceiling.

A Well-Lit Kitchen

A kitchen can be fitted with the finest of materials and the latest appliances, but it'll be a dismal place if badly lit day or night. Lighting makes a radical difference in how easy—and pleasant—it is to cook, eat, clean up, and socialize. For much of the day direct and diffuse sunlight add warmth and atmosphere, especially welcome in the morning. If light is prized but heat is not, consider seasonal shading by way of overhangs and trees, and install interior shades or curtains.

Regardless of how much natural light your kitchen receives, artificial light is crucial as well. Task lighting is essential for safe and pleasant cooking, while ambient lighting is essential for well-being, and well-placed accent lighting provides the garnish. All kitchens—especially those that open to the dining room or family room—will benefit from lighting that's adjustable. If task, ambient, and ornamental lighting are wired separately, an adjacent dinner party can be bathed with light while scullery work stays in shadow. Carefully zoned lighting, along with economical light fixtures, can reduce your electrical bill, too.

◀ **A BALANCE OF TONES AND LIGHT SOURCES** makes this a beautifully lit kitchen. The high ceilng is darker to keep it from floating away, and the porthole window is deep to make for more diffuse light. Tiny halogen downlights are recessed in soffits for task and ambient lighting. The dishwashing workspace is bumped out to provide a corner full of windows.

Natural Light

Windows enlarge a kitchen by extending the view, and add a quality of light that artificial fixtures can't match. Guidelines suggest that windows equal 10 percent of the floor area, but that's a bare—and dark—minimum. The trend to replace wall cabinets with windows makes for a brighter kitchen.

How a kitchen is oriented affects window size and placement. North light can be pleasantly diffuse for working at a countertop. South-facing windows provide solar heating in winter months when the sun is lower in the sky. To keep out summer heat, provide a deep roof overhang or shades. Windows facing east or west are a mixed blessing. Morning sun can be a delight, but west-facing windows need shades to lessen the glare of afternoon sun. Windows on facing or intersecting walls make light that's brighter yet less glaring than a single, large window. Windows close to a wall, ceiling, or countertop bounce light off those surfaces.

▼ WALL-TO-WALL, BACKSPLASH-TO-CEILING GLASS allows a full view of the woods from this kitchen. Glass panels are joined simply at the corner. It's a more fragile detail than fitting window frames into a standard wall, but it really brings in the outdoors.

◀ THIS 2-FT. BY 6-FT. SKYLIGHT WELL HAS SPLAYED sides to reflect light throughout the kitchen. The skylight is glazed with a double layer of translucent fiberglass panels. Low-voltage halogen fixtures slide on a curved track for easy adjustments.

▼ A SOUTH-FACING CLERESTORY WINDOW above this dining area allows sunlight to bounce off the upper wall and diffuse throughout the space. Randomly placed glass blocks bring in more soft light in an artful way.

◀ THIS BAY OF NARROW, DOUBLE-HUNG WINDOWS is supplemented by windows on the adjacent wall, making a light-filled, cheerful kitchen that's easy to work in. Tiny low-voltage halogens and recessed downlights dramatically light the kitchen at night.

A Well-Lit Kitchen | 171

▲ THIS DINING AREA DIRECTLY OFF THE KITCHEN is defined by an octagonal coved ceiling with dimmable perimeter lighting, a pendant light, and windows that let in a phenomenal view.

▶ MORNING LIGHT IS WELCOME IN THIS COUNTRY HOUSE, so the narrow window above the range isn't fitted with shades. The south-facing window over the sink does have protection from a porch overhang. Lighting is provided by pendants, recessed downlights, and range-hood lights.

▲A REDESIGNED WINDOW ON A WEST-FACING WALL helps soften the afternoon sun. The whole window area was bumped out and framed at the top with a steel angle that takes up less room than the old 2x wood header. A glass-block panel and new casements set at the outside edge of the bump-out help screen the setting sun.

◄SKYLIGHTS ON BOTH SIDES OF A GABLED ROOF brighten this kitchen in the woods; trees help keep sunlight diffuse. At night, sconces shine on the gable end and sides, and the yellow paint keeps the ambience warm.

Supplemental Lighting

MAKE MOST KITCHEN LIGHTING TASK LIGHTING. Position task lighting in front of you by using undercabinet lights, adjustable wall-mounted fixtures, or downlights 10 in. to 12 in. from wall cabinets. Ambient light is best when diffuse, as its job is to brighten the kitchen overall. It can come from a central fixture, downlights, well-placed and abundant above-cabinet fixtures, or several sources at once. Fixtures that bounce light off ceilings and walls are more efficient than recessed downlights, which can leave the ceiling dark. Accent lighting adds ambience.

Different sources of light make for a more versatile kitchen. Wiring groups of light fixtures separately allows a kitchen to multitask, especially with dimming controls. Be aware that dark surfaces absorb light and glossy surfaces make sharp reflections. Light, matte surfaces reflect light diffusely.

▼ SEVERAL TYPES OF LIGHTS GIVE THIS KITCHEN the look of a train car. Surface-mounted ceiling lights add a decorative touch to the ceiling, while a smaller surface-mounted fixture punctuates the line above the door. More modest, small downlights provide task lighting, supplemented by undercabinet lighting and a window.

◄ THERE'S NO POINT IN HAVING A TALL CEILING without making use of that extra space above the cabinets. Adding this curved-top clerestory window makes the window at the sink extraordinary, while the windows above the cabinets on each side bounce light off the ceiling.

▼ CORNER WINDOWS DOUBLE THE BRIGHTNESS in this kitchen by bouncing light off three surfaces. Each window has a complementary light above so that at night light will come from the same place. Copper pendants and wall-mounted fixtures provide additional lighting. Undercabinet lights supplement task lighting.

▶ THIS WOOD-FILLED KITCHEN GETS ABUNDANT DAYLIGHT, which is supplemented by several pendant incandescent light fixtures to ensure adequate lighting at night or on gloomy days. The undercabinet lighting is switched at the fixture rather than at the wall, which makes the switch less visible but also a bit harder to locate.

About Bulbs

WHILE THE STYLE OF FIXTURE YOU CHOOSE influences the look of a kitchen, the type of bulb used gives the overall luminescent effect. Use the following as a guide to choosing the best lighting sources for your needs.

Incandescent bulbs comprise a large category that includes any type with a filament, including standard tungsten and halogen bulbs. However, the standard incandescent bulb, called an A-type bulb, is what we'll discuss here. Although it costs little, it's expensive to operate because it is inefficient and short-lived (only 10% of the energy generated from an incandescent bulb produces light; the rest is heat). Incandescents remain popular because the warm color is flattering to people and food and they are easy to dim. But halogen, xenon, and new, improved fluorescent bulbs are changing people's buying habits.

Fluorescent bulbs are cooler than incandescent bulbs, four times as efficient, and last ten times longer. Forget the ghastly green fluorescents in your elementary school classroom, or even that old 2-ft. fluorescent in an overhead kitchen fixture—today's residential fluorescent bulbs can be compact enough for use in recessed downlights, in lamps, and under cabinets, and, even better, they can make people and food look natural. Color is measured by the Color Rendering Index (CRI) figure, which rates how realistic objects will look under that light, or the Kelvin rating, which measures color temperature. Look for a CRI of 82 or above or a Kelvin rating of 3,000K or lower.

The compact fluorescent lamp (CFL) has been a major boost to saving energy. These bulbs are roughly the same size as an A-type incandescent, so you can relamp many incandescent fixtures with CFLs. CFLs are expensive, but many electrical utility companies offer rebates or fixtures themselves at lower cost. In any case, CFLs can save 75 percent per fixture and they last ten times as long as incandescent bulbs.

◄ A COMBINATION OF BULB TYPES MAKES FOR VERSATILE lighting. Incandescent downlights and fluorescent under-cabinet lights combine to provide task lighting and ambient light. White blinds help reflect light from wall-washer downlights, and the light stone tiles magnify the amount of light given off by the undercabinet lights.

◄ THESE PETITE HALOGEN PEN-
DANTS ARE HUNG by black wires
that mimic the black cables tying
the roof together. Although these
are low voltage, halogen bulbs
provide a powerful amount of
light for their size, and their color
mimics daylight.

▼ SURFACE-MOUNTED INCANDES-
CENT FIXTURES with translucent
lenses and low-voltage halogen
pendants provide abundant task
and ambient light, supplementing
the ribbon of windows in this
bright kitchen. Both incandescent
and halogen bulbs are easy to
dim, so the ambience can change
with the time of day and task
at hand.

Halogen bulbs are relatively expensive but put out
more light than incandescents and have exceptional color
rendition and beam control, making them all-around can-
didates for ambient and task lighting. Halogen bulbs are
available in line-volt fixtures (120 volt) or low-voltage fixtures (12 volt). Low-voltage halogens, found in miniature
recessed downlights and undercabinet lights, require a
transformer to step down from line voltage. Xenon lamps,
the new kids on the block, are touted as being cooler and
longer lasting than halogens, but they still run warmer and
are less efficient than fluorescents.

Don't be tempted to ignore that little label inside a recessed light fixture that indicates the maximum wattage.
It's safer to have more fixtures than risk the fire hazard of
using a bulb that's too hot for the fixture.

WINDOWS CARVED INTO THE STAINLESS-STEEL BACKSPLASH brighten an urban kitchen, while low-voltage halogen lighting supplies sparkle. A low-voltage monorail track system holds adjustable fixtures. The suspended plate over the cooktop and matching ledge atop the wall cabinets hold individual halogens. Undercabinet fixtures boost task lighting.

AN ARCHED TRELLIS MAKES A STYLISH SCREEN BETWEEN kitchen and dining room, and it's a clever place to hang halogen lights. During the day light streams in from kitchen and dining room windows.

Dimming Lights

DIMMING LIGHT FIXTURES CAN CHANGE MOOD, make lighting options more flexible, and reduce energy use (on occasion, halogen lights should be run at full brightness for a few minutes to preserve lamp life). Different scenarios have different lighting needs, easily handled by dimming light fixtures. At dinner the center of the table should be lit, as if from a campfire. When you are making dinner, light the perimeter of the kitchen so that work can be done. Integrated dimming systems allow you to preset various lighting scenarios that can be called up with the touch of a button or with a remote-control device.

Undercabinet Lighting

U NDERCABINET LIGHTING **can provide the brightest task lighting on countertops, as it's situated directly over and fairly close to the work surface. Halogen puck lights or thin tubes, flexible rope lights, and pencil-thin fluorescent tubes with or without lenses are popular choices for undercabinet fixtures. Some fixtures allow for the first unit to be hardwired while adjacent fixtures plug one into the next. Maintaining a low profile is important, and a valence added to or designed into cabinets will help hide fixtures. Keeping the fixture close to the front of the cabinet helps conceal the fixture and will cause less glare on the countertop.**

▲ HIDDEN LIGHT SOURCES ARE THE KEY IN THIS KITCHEN. The ceiling grid adds texture and a place to tuck panels of tiny lights, while undercabinet and over-sink lighting is concealed by cabinets and valences.

◄ LIGHTING IS BOTH SUBTLE AND SHOWY in this high-ceilinged kitchen. A two-light pendant brings light to the island countertop. Range-hood lights illuminate both cooking tasks and a decorative tile backsplash. Adjustable recessed halogen downlights highlight the bay-window wall.

▶ THIS PATTERNED STAINLESS-STEEL DOOR LIFTS UP to display an array of small appliances. A ribbon of tiny lights illuminates the interior for easier access. The cabinet also holds a bank of receptacles.

▼ DOWNLIGHTS WERE NOT PART OF THE DESIGN PALETTE in this Craftsman-style kitchen, so surface-mounted, period-style fixtures fit the bill.

Lighting Inside Cabinets

CABINETS WITH GLASS DOORS **always benefit from inside lighting—use glass shelves, too, for extra sparkle. Low-voltage light fixtures, such as puck lights and rope lights, work well inside cabinets because they are small. Low-voltage fixtures can be operated by a touch switch or with wiring affixed to a hinge or hidden metal strip so that lights turn on automatically when the door is opened. Another candidate for cabinet lighting is the notoriously dark and difficult-to-rummage-through corner base cabinet.**

▲ THE MINIATURE STRIP LIGHTS IN THESE GLASS CABINETS and the strip halogens in the toespace provide a dramatic glow in the evening, after kitchen work is done.

Locating Pendants

LIGHTING AN ISLAND OR PENINSULA **with pendant lighting can provide both task and ambient lighting, and a translucent shade will add soft light to the ceiling, too. Keep the bottom of a pendant at about 36 in. above an island and 30 in. above a dining table—44 in. to 50 in. if the ceiling is especially high. Measure well to assure that the fixture is within the boundaries of the table or island. A pendant fixture is especially pleasing if it can be dimmed.**

▲ EACH OF THE CEILING LAYERS IN THIS KITCHEN is fitted with white-trimmed recessed downlights for maximum visual impact and illumination. Additional lighting is supplied by two pendants over the island and by undercabinet lighting.

▶ IN THIS TEXAS HILL COUNTRY HOUSE, deep overhangs are critical for keeping out the sun and glare. The window over the refrigerator faces south, but the window is small. Low-voltage lights provide a cheerful glow at the sink.

Recessed Downlights

DOWNLIGHTS ARE PERFECT FOR ALL KITCHEN TASKS, including washing surfaces of wall cabinets and walls, adding task lighting to countertops, providing ambient light, and accenting decorative objects. But use them with care. Take a look at the size, configuration, and color of the trim and select the bulb that provides the beam spread and illumination level you need. Also pay attention to where downlights are positioned. A downlight that's out of line with its neighbors will forever make you wince. Choose recessed fixtures that are as airtight as possible to reduce heat loss and keep moisture from migrating into the attic or a wall cavity; select IC-type fixtures for contact with insulation.

For accent lighting, consider adjustable lenses or lamps with narrow beams. To minimize the look of downlights, use the much smaller low-voltage downlight lamps, which have apertures as small as 2 in. Look for trims that match the ceiling or frosted lenses that cover the bulb.

Supplement downlights with sconces or other sources of uplighting to keep the ceiling from looking dark. Some homeowners avoid downlights and prefer to go with pendants, sconces, swing-arm fixtures, and other surface-mounted or suspended fixtures.

▲ SOFFITS CAN BE A HANDY LOCATION FOR RECESSED downlights and help bring the light closer to working surfaces. While downlights provide task lighting over the peninsula, glass-shaded pendants add flair and lightness.

THESE HALOGEN LIGHTS ARE DESIGNED TO BE SEEN rather than hidden. The four semirecessed fixtures add sparkle to cabinets that open from both sides. Three halogen fixtures create task lighting for the countertop.

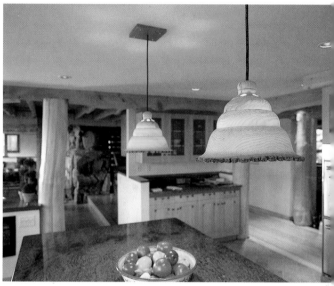

LIGHT FIXTURES OVER A KITCHEN ISLAND are made from wood turned on a lathe, in keeping with Southwest and Japanese-style designs found throughout this Vermont timber-frame house.

IN THIS CITY KITCHEN AN OPAQUE ROMAN SHADE keeps out glaring western sun in the summer and provides privacy at night. Surface-mounted halogens provide night-time task lighting over the sink, while undercabinet puck lights provide day and night task lighting on countertops.

▶ LIGHTING UPPER CABINETS IS COMMON, but why not light base cabinets that face the dining area, too? This top-lit island cabinet has glass shelves that allow light to bounce around.

▼ THIS BROOKLYN CARRIAGE HOUSE WAS RENOVATED to reflect its mixed residential and industrial neighborhood. In keeping with the industrial setting, the architect designed a pendant light fixture with metal tubing, small halogen reflectors, and a metal frame carrying a curved plastic lens that diffuses light.

Fitting in Receptacles

FINDING A PLACE FOR ELECTRICAL OUTLETS shouldn't be an afterthought. To minimize the effect of receptacles, try to cluster them behind where appliances will sit, or camouflage covers with faux painting or matching material. Another alternative is to tuck plug molding (also called strip receptacles) under wall cabinets (keep in mind that cords will hang down from under the cabinet). Both plug molding and receptacles can become a design feature with stainless steel or decorative plates.

Receptacles in islands can not be placed face up, nor be placed under an overhang deeper than a few inches. If your island has two countertop levels, you've got a built-in backsplash, perfect for receptacles and safer than below the countertop because cords won't be hanging over the countertop. Sans backsplash, an island can be designed with decorative legs that incorporate receptacles so that you don't lose precious storage space to an electrical box. Building codes usually require ground-fault circuit interrupter (GFCI) receptacles in kitchens, not just around the sink.

▶ IT'S TOUGH TO FIND A PLACE FOR RECEPTACLES in an island, as there's no backsplash and space is packed with drawers or appliances. Here, a strip of easy-to-reach plug molding fits below the countertop. Box beams provide not only a sheltering look but utility, as halogen lights are recessed into the undersides.

Sources

In the search for kitchen information there is much treasure to be had if you dig in the right places. Books can be read, reread, covered with sticky notes, and hauled from place to place. Magazines are good sources, not just for articles and product source lists, but also for ads showing the latest products. The Web is, well, a web, with both threads of gold and threads woven into the emperor's new clothes. Keep in mind that there is no global fact checker, nor are sources always attributed properly. The best resource is actual experience. Go cook on the range you covet, go to a stone yard and touch that granite you've only seen in photographs. You can get vicarious experience from Web forums (see below). All of these sources require a filter, and that filter is your own good sense.

Taunton Press Publications

I admit my bias for Taunton Press publications—I've subscribed to *Fine Homebuilding* since issue 4 and refuse to lend a single copy. And, of course, this is a Taunton book. Nonetheless, Taunton is a great resource for anyone doing new-kitchen research. Look to Taunton books and magazines for design inspiration, for help in choosing kitchen stuff, and for hands-on just about every aspect of making kitchens.

Look especially for the *Fine Homebuilding* annual *Kitchen & Baths* issues, which come out once a year in the fall. These magazines are keepers. Each issue has one or two articles about choosing kitchen elements, along with several featured kitchens with in-depth info about design and materials.

There are many Taunton books that involve kitchens; here are just a few:

Cheng, Fu-Tung, with Eric Olsen. *Concrete Countertops.* Newtown, CT: The Taunton Press, 2002.
Handsome enough for the coffee table and useful enough to hold open with a length of rebar as you form a countertop, this book offers a combination of inspirational and hands-on expertise in making precast concrete countertops (there is an appendix about a cast-in-place countertop). Cheng is an artist and concrete is his means of expression. His passion for concrete will get you thinking, "I can do this, too!" It is not as easy as it looks, but Cheng is upfront about concrete's temperamental nature.

Susanka, Sarah. *Not So Big Solutions for Your Home, Not So Big House, Creating the Not So Big House, The Not So Big House Collection.* Newtown, CT: The Taunton Press.

Web Sites

The Web has completely changed the way we do research on kitchen design and building, for homeowners, designers, and builders. You can buy anything, from a knob to expertise. As with all purchases and all advice, let the buyer beware. Web sites run by nonprofit organizations can offer lots of information without advertising, but don't expect objectivity, as every source has a point of view. Many Web site's FAQ pages and links to other Web sites can be good sources of information.

Here are some sites I've found interesting or useful—and sometimes both:

americanlightingassoc.com
Links to lighting consultants and showrooms and provides lighting tips and information.

www.appliance.com
This site offers appliance buyer's guides (written by manufacturers), lists of suppliers, and links to appliance repair sources, energy suppliers, and government agencies.

www.build.com
This "'Building and Home Improvement Directory" has been around since 1994, offering links to manufacturers of building products, online merchants of home products, building publications, and a big list of builders, designers, real estate agents, and mortgage brokers.

www.energystar.gov
This government agency manages the ENERGY STAR program that cites appliances that exceed federal efficiency standards. You can find appliances that make the cut as well as the stores that carry them.

www.hgtv.com
This good-looking site offers a detailed program guide to the Home & Garden television show, short video tips, DIY projects, crafts, and message boards.

www.homeportfolio.com
A directory of home products offered by registered manufacturers and retailers, a designer directory, message boards, and articles about design, lighting, and cabinet layout.

www.ifloor.com
This site bills itself as "the Internet's Flooring Store," and it carries just about every floor type you could imagine for a kitchen. I haven't bought flooring here, but I've made use of their detailed information about flooring types and installation.

www.kitchens.com
The National Kitchen and Bath Association operates this site geared to the consumer. It has guidelines for design—look for the NKBA's 40 kitchen-layout guidelines as well as guides to choosing appliances, countertops, floors, and other kitchen elements.

http://oikos.com
Oikos means "house" in Greek and is the root of "ecology" and "economy." This Web site, subtitled "Green Building Source," is aimed at professionals, but it includes links to sustainable materials and products and energy-efficient publications and news.

www.period-homes.com
This Web site is run by *Period Homes* Magazine, one of Clem Labine's resourceful publications (*Clem Labine's Traditional Building* focuses on commercial and civic projects, but it's relevant to houses, too). It provides links to the actual Web sites of manufacturers who make products for pre-1940 houses and new homes built in traditional styles.

www.superkitchens.com
This site has lots of design info about materials, layouts, and trends, all from the viewpoint of its owner, KraftMaid Cabinetry, Inc.

www.taunton.com
Start here to go to The Taunton Press, *Fine Homebuilding, Fine Woodworking,* and *Fine Cooking,* where you'll find Web extras, a few posted articles from the magazines, and links to an ever-growing list of manufacturers, publications about building, and information sites. Don't bypass the forums—"Breaktime" for *Fine Homebuilding,* "Knots" for *Fine Woodworking,* and "Cook's Talk" for *Fine Cooking—where you can get advice about everything involving kitchens. You won't find a richer source of opinions on building than the generous and ardent regulars at "Breaktime," nor will you find a more passionate discussion of gas versus electric cooktops than on the Web pages of "Cook's Talk."

Credits

p. 98: Photo: © Brian Vanden Brink, Photographer 2004.

p. 99: (right) Design: Rob Thallon, Eugene, OR, Photo: © The Taunton Press, Inc.; (left) Design: Morningstar Marble & Granite, Inc., Topsham, ME, Photo: © Brian Vanden Brink, Photographer 2004.

p. 100: (top left) Design: T-1, Photo: © Jason McConathy; (top right) Design: Brian Cooper, builder, Photo: © Brian Vanden Brink, Photographer 2004; (bottom) Design: Scott Ballard, Houston, TX, Photo: © The Taunton Press Inc.

p. 101: Design: Rob Thallon, Eugene, OR, Photo: © The Taunton Press, Inc.

p. 102: Design: Weston Hewitson Architects Inc., Hingham, MA, Photo: © Brian Vanden Brink, Photographer 2004.

p.103 (top) Photo: © Brian Vanden Brink, Photographer 2004; (bottom) Design: John Malick, Emeryville, CA, Photo: © The Taunton Press, Inc.

p. 104: (top) Design: Dan Scully, Architect, Photo: © Brian Vanden Brink, Photographer 2004;(bottom) Design: GKW Working Design, Stowe, VT, Photo: © 2004 carolynbates.com.

p. 105: Design: Jon Dick, ARCHAEO, Santa Fe, NM, Photo: © The Taunton Press, Inc.

p. 106: (left) Design: Mark Mulligan, Cambridge, MA, Photo: Chris Green; (right) Photo: © Steve Rosenthal.

p. 107 Design: Nina Birnbaum and Clem Donahue, Photo: © The Taunton Press, Inc.

p. 108 (left and right) Design: Frank Karreman, Bainbridge, WA, Photo: © The Taunton Press.

p. 109: (top) Design: Nina Birnbaum and Clem Donahue, Photo: © The Taunton Press, Inc.; (bottom) Design: Frost Cabinets, St. Paul, MN, Cabinet finish: Kim Sheridan, MN, Photo: © The Taunton Press, Inc.

p. 110: Design: Woodstock Kitchens & Baths, Essex Junction, VT, Photo: © 2004 carolynbates.com.

p. 111: (left) Photo: © Jason McConathy; (right) Design: Drysdale Associates, Interior Design, Photo: © Brian Vanden Brink, Photographer 2004.

p. 112: (top) Design: Diane Morgan, Portland, OR, Photo: © The Taunton Press, Inc.; (bottom) Design: Morningstar Marble & Granite, Inc., Topsham, ME, Photo: © Brian Vanden Brink, Photographer 2004.

p. 113: Design: Jim Garramone, Evanston, Il, Photo: © The Taunton Press, Inc.

p. 114: Photo: © Jason McConathy.

p. 115: (top) Design: Molli Moran, MA, Photo: © 2004 carolynbates.com; (bottom) Design: Andre Rothblatt, San Francisco, CA, Photo: © The Taunton Press, Inc.

p. 116: Design: Pete de Girolamo, Salerno, Livingston Architects; Connie de Griolamo, San Diego, CA, Photo: © The Taunton Press, Inc.

p. 117: (top) Photo: © Jason McConathy; (bottom) Design: Roc Calvano Architect, Bar Harbour, ME, Photo: © Brian Vanden Brink, Photographer 2004.

CHAPTER 5

p. 118 Design: Kaehler Moore Architects, Greenwich, CT, Photo: © H. Durston Saylor.

p. 120: Photo: © Jason McConathy.

p. 121: (top) Design: Damian Baumhover, San Diego, Ca, Photo: © The Taunton Press, Inc.; (bottom) Photo: © Jason McConathy.

p. 122: (top) Photo: © Jason McConathy; (bottom) Design: Frost Cabinets, St. Paul, MN, Cabinet finish: Kim Sheridan, MN, Photo: © The Taunton Press, Inc.

p. 123: (top left) Diane Morgan with architect Margie Sanders, Portland, OR, Cabinetmaker: Simon, Toney and Fisher, Portland, OR, Concrete counters: Eric Butler, Lighting: Paul Scardina; (right) Jim Garramone, Evanston, IL, Photo: © The Taunton Press, Inc. (bottom left) Design: Rothchild, Photo: © Brian Vanden Brink, Photographer 2004.

p. 124: (top) Design: Roland Batten Architect/ Linda Reeve MacIntyre, Shelburne, VT, Photo: © 2004 carolynbates.com; (bottom) Design: Malcom Appleton, Architectural Association & Barbara Strattas, Waitsfield, VT, Photo: © 2004 carolynbates.com.

p. 125: (top) Design: Anne Otterson, owner, Robert Mosher, architect, La Jolla, CA, Photo: © The Taunton Press, Inc.; (bottom) Photo: © 2004 carolynbates.com.

p. 126: (top) Design: Vermont Vernacular, East Calais, VT, Photo: © 2004 carolynbates.com, (bottom) Design: Dana Ennis, Ascutney, VT, Photo: © 2004 carolynbates.com.

p. 127: (top) Design: Oliver 2, Photo: © Brian Vanden Brink, Photographer 2004; (center) Design: J. Graham Goldsmith Architects PC, Burlington, VT, Photo: © 2004 carolynbates.com, (bottom) Design: Brad Rabinowitz, Architect, Burlington, VT, Photo: © 2004 carolynbates.com.

p. 128: (left) Design: Nason Singer, Laughing Bear Associates, Montpelier, VT, Photo: © 2004 carolynbates.com; (top right) Design: Cushman & Beckman, Stowe, VT, Photo: © 2004 carolynbates.com, (bottom right) Photo: © Jason McConathy.

p. 129: Design: Woodstock Kitchens & Baths, Essex Junction, VT, Photo: © 2004 carolynbates.com.

p. 130: (top) Design: Diane Morgan, Photo: © The Taunton Press, Inc.; (bottom) Design: Frank W. Riepe, Sudbury, MA, Photo: © The Taunton Press, Inc.

p. 131: (top) Design: Mildord Cushman, Cushman + Beckstrom, Inc., Stowe, VT and Rockport, ME, Photo: © 2004 carolynbates.com; (bottom) Photo: © Jason McConathy.

p. 132: (top) Design: Earthstone Stove, Architect: Shahin Barzin, Photo: © The Taunton Press; (bottom left) Design: Jim Huntington, Charlotte, VT, Photo: © 2004 carolynbates.com; (bottom right) Interior design: Marlene Chargin, Fresno, CA; Kitchen design: De Ann Martin; Builder: Mark Fletcher, Madera, CA; Warming oven: Dacor; Photo: © The Taunton Press, Inc.

p. 133: (top) Design: David Luce, Wilson Architects, Waterbury, VT, Photo: © 2004 carolynbates.com; (bottom) Design: Kenneth Bennett, Essex, Junction, VT and Larry Kruse, North Woods Joinery, Jeffersonville, VT, Photo: © 2004 carolynbates.com.

p.134: Photo: © Jason McConathy.

p. 135: (top left) Design: Robson Bilgen Architects, Hancock,VT, Photo: © 2004 carolynbates.com; (bottom left) Photo: © Jason McConathy; (right) Design: John Malick, Emeryville, CA, Photo: © The Taunton Press.

p. 136: (top) Photo: © Brian Vanden Brink, Photographer 2004; (bottom) Peter Morris Architects, Vergennes, VT, Photo: © 2004 carolynbates.com.

p. 137: (left) Architect: Roland Batten, Builder: John Seibert, Birdseye Building Company, Richmond VT, Photo: © The Taunton Press, Inc.; (right) Cabinetmaker: Thompson & Brouillette Inc., Providence, RI, Architect: Shahin Barzin, Providence, RI, Photo: © The Taunton Press.

p. 138: (top) Design: Ron and Patricia Ryan Madson, El Granada, CA, Cooktop: DCS, Rangehood: WindCraft, Photo: © The Taunton Press, Inc.; (bottom) Photo: © 2004 carolynbates.com.

p. 140: (left) Design: Jim Bischoff, Photo: © The Taunton Press, Inc.; (top right) Design: Weston Hewitson Architects Inc., Hingham, MA, © Brian Vanden Brink, Photographer 2004; (bottom right) Design: Neilson & Taylor, Photo: © Brian Vanden Brink, Photographer 2004.

p. 141: (left) Design; John Martin, Builder: Tim Bullock, Photo: © Brian Vanden Brink, Photographer 2004; (right) Design: Jim Huntington, Charlotte, VT, Photo: © 2004 carolynbates.com.

p. 142: Michael Dugan, Essex Junction, VT, Photo: © 2004 carolynbates.com.

p. 143: (top) Design: Noel Tewes, Bangor, ME and Laurel Tewes, Great Barrington, MA, Photo: © 2004 carolynbates.com; (bottom) Photo: © Jason McConathy.

p. 144: (top) Photo: © Jason McConathy; (bottom) Design: David Rogers, AuSable Valley Woodworks, Keesville, NY, Photo:© Nancie Battaglia.

p. 145 (top) Photo: © Jason McConathy; (bottom) Design: Bentley & Churchill Architects, Siaconset, MA, Refrigerators: Sub-Zero, Photo: Tim O'Brien.

p. 146: (top left) Design: Shiloh Millworks, Phoenix, AZ, Photo: © Robert Romaneck, Shiloh Millworks, Scottsdale, AZ, Photo by Steve Thompson; (top right) Design: Taos Red Cabinet & Construction Co., Inc., El Prado, NM, © 2004 Terry Thompson; (bottom) Design: brooksBerry Associates, St. Louis, MO; (bottom) Photo: © Alison O'Brien photography.

p. 147: (top) Design: Hutner/Rollnick, Photo: © Brian Vanden Brink, Photographer 2004; (bottom) Design: John Martin, Builder: Tim Bullock, Photo: © Brian Vanden Brink, Photographer 2004.

CHAPTER 6

p. 148: Design: Frost Cabinets, St. Paul, MN, Photo: © The Taunton Press, Inc.

p. 150: Photo : © Randy O'Rourke.

p. 151: (top) Photo: © Steve Rosenthal; (bottom) Design: Ed Pierce and Jan Goodrich, Bennington, VT.

p. 152: Design: Thunder Mill Design, Montpelier, VT.

p. 153: Design: Rob Hetler, Cabinetmaker, Greenbank, WA, Photo: © Bill Ruth.

p. 154: Design: Elliott & Elliott Architects, Photo: © Brian Vanden Brink, Photographer 2004.

p. 155: Design: Craftsmen Unlimited, Inc., Burlington, VT, Photo: © 2004 carolynbates.com.

p. 156: (left) Photo: © 2004 carolynbates.com; (top right) Design: Phillips Wolcott, Architect, Stowe, VT; (bottom right) Design: Brad Rabinowitz, Architect, Burlington, VT, Photo: © 2004 carolynbates.com.

p. 158: (left) Jane Langmuir, Interior Design, Providence, RI, Photo: © Brian Vanden Brink, Photographer 2004; (top right) Photo: © Jason McConathy; (bottom right) Design: Peter Rose, Architect, Photo: © Brian Vanden Brink, Photographer 2004.

p. 159: (left) Design: Mac White from Michael G. Imber, Architect, San Antonio, TX, Photo: © The Taunton Press, Inc.; (right) Design: Brad Rabinowitz, Architect, Burlington, VT, Photo: © 2004 carolynbates.com.

p. 160: Design: Damian Baumhover, San Diego, CA, Photo: © The Taunton Press, Inc.

p. 161: (left) Design: Houses & Barns by John Libby, Photo: © Brian Vanden Brink, Photographer 2004; (right) Design: Jerry Thompson.

p. 162: (left) Design: Mostue & Associates, Architecture, Inc., Photo: © Steve Rosenthal; (right) Design: David Lyon for Colleen Horner Kitchen Bath Tile Stone, Pewaukee, WI, Photo: © Alison O'Brien photography.

p. 163: Design: Paul Duncker and Peggy Dunker, Jackson Hole, WY, Photo: © The Taunton Press, Inc.

p. 164: Photo: © Aaron Pennock.

p. 165: (top) Design: David Coleman, Seattle, WA, Photo: © 2004 carolynbates.com; (bottom) Photo: © 2004 carolynbates.com.

p. 166: (left) Design: Scholz & Barclay Architects, Photo: © Brian Vanden Brink, Photographer 2004; (top right) Photo: © 2004 carolynbates.com; (bottom right) Design: South Mountain Company, Martha's Vineyard, MA, Photo: © Brian Vanden Brink, Photographer 2004.

p. 167: (top left) Design: Pete de Girolamo, Salerno, Livingston Architects; San Diego, CA, Photo: © The Taunton Press, Inc.; (bottom left) Photo: © Brian Vanden Brink, Photographer 2004; (right) Design: Jim Garramone, Evanston, IL, Photo: © The Taunton Press, Inc.

CHAPTER 7

p. 168: Design: Mark Hutker & Associates Architects, Inc., Vineyard Haven and Falmouth, MA, Photo: © Brian Vanden Brink, Photographer 2004.

p. 170: Photo: © 2004 carolynbates.com.

p. 171: (top left) Interior Design: Marlene Chargin, Fresno, CA, Kitchen Design: De Ann Martin, Builder: Mark Fletcher, Madera, CA, Cabinets: Prémoule, Ontario, Canada, Photo: © The Taunton Press, Inc; (bottom left) Photo: © Jason McConathy; (right) Berry Lanford, Albuquerque, NM, Photo: © The Taunton Press, Inc.

p. 172: (left) Design: Dominic Mercandante, Belfast, ME, Photo: © Brian Vanden Brink, Photographer 2004; (right) Design: Mark Hutker & Associates Architects, Inc., Vineyard Haven and Falmouth, MA, Photo: © Brian Vanden Brink, Photographer 2004.

p. 173: (top) Design:Frank W. Riepe, Sudbury, MA, Photo: © The Taunton Press, Inc.; (bottom) Design: Mostue Y Associates, Architects, Inc., Somerville, MA, Photo: © Steve Rosenthal.

p. 174: Design: Mildord Cushman, Cushman + Beckstrom, Inc., Stowe, VT and Rockport, ME, Photo: © 2004 carolynbates.com.

p. 175: (top left) Design: F-1, Photo: © Jason McConathy; (bottom left) Design: Roland Batten, Shelburne, VT, Photo: © 2004 carolynbates.com; (right) Design: H. H. Benedict, Shaftsbury, VT, Photo: © 2004 carolynbates.com.

p. 176: Design: Nancy McCoy, Lighting Designer, San Francisco, CA, Photo: © The Taunton Press.

p. 177: (top) Photo: © Jason McConathy; (bottom) Design: Mark Hutker & Associates, Inc., Vineyard Haven and Falmouth, MA, Photo: © Brian Vanden Brink, Photographer 2004.

p. 178: (left) Design: brooksBerry and Associates Kitchens and Baths, St. Loiuis, MO, Photo: © Alison O'Brien photography; (right) Photo: © Jason McConathy.

p. 179: (left) Design: Axel Berg, Builder, Photo: © Brian Vanden Brink, Photographer 2004; (right) Design: John Morris, Camden, ME, Photo: © Brian Vanden Brink, Photographer 2004.

p. 180: (top) Design: Diane Morgan, owner; Margie Sanders, architect, Portland, OR, Cabinetmakers: Simon, Toney and Fischer, Photo: © The Taunton Press, Inc., (bottom left) Design: Pete de Girolamo, Salerno, Livingston Architects; San Diego, CA, Photo: © The Taunton Press, Inc. (bottom right) Design: Nancy McCoy, Lighting Designer, San Francisco, CA, Photo: © The Taunton Press.

p. 181: (left) Design: Brad Rabinowitz, Architect, Burlington, VT, Photo: © The Taunton Press, Inc.; (right) Design: Mac White from Michael G. Imber, Architect, San Antonio, TX, Photo: © The Taunton Press, Inc.

p. 182: Design: Mark Hutker & Associates Architects, Inc., Vineyard Haven and Falmouth, MA, Photo: © Brian Vanden Brink, Photographer 2004.

p. 183: (top left) Design: Damian Baumhover, San Diego, CA, Photo: © The Taunton Press, Inc.; (bottom left) Photo © davidduncanlivingston.com; (right) Design: Kate Stevens, Sellers and Company Architects, Warren, VT, Photo: © The Taunton Press.

p. 184: (top) Photo © davidduncanlivingston.com; (bottom) Design: Coburn Architecture, Brooklyn, NY, Photo: © The Taunton Press, Inc.

p. 185: Design: Van Dam Architecture and design, Portland, ME, Photo: © Brian Vanden Brink, Photographer 2004.